THE LONDON Q

THE LONDON Q

KEN BLACKER

Capital Transport

First published 2022

ISBN 978-1-85414-470-6

Published by Capital Transport Publishing Ltd
www.capitaltransport.com

Printed by Parksons Graphics

CONTENTS

INTRODUCTION

The AEC Q-type was one of the more interesting and unusual passenger vehicle designs of the inter-war years and much has already been written about it, most notably by the late Alan Townsin whose book entitled 'The AEC Q Family' was published as part of the 'Best of British Buses' series in 1981. In truth, it was probably a great exaggeration to deem the AEC Q as one of the best of British buses, as it was far from perfect, but nevertheless it served London and the inner home counties well for almost two decades, flooding on to the streets in 1935/36 and disappearing almost as rapidly in 1952/53. Uniquely, the Q designation used by AEC was also used as a class description by London Transport who amassed a fleet of 238 Qs. London Transport was, in fact, the only operator with whom the Q really gained any substantial foothold, which this volume sets out to describe.

The prototype Q 1, and the handful of double deckers, had all gone before I had a chance to see them, but I remember the bulk of the fleet very well and travelled on them on many occasions. When I was a boy, living in north London, Q types were part of my everyday world. In bus format they were the staple diet on my local single deck service, West Green garage's local route 233, while the coach version based at Guildford and Hertford passed through every 20 minutes on the very busy Green Line 715. I quite warmed to the bus version (which I later learned was known in the business as the 5Q5) even though it looked like no other single deckers in the red bus fleet and seemed more prone to knocks and dents than other types, and I really admired the comfort and modern-ness of its interior. On the other hand I found the coaches (6Q6s) unappealingly bulky and ungainly in appearance, and positively lacking in style compared with the far more ubiquitous Green Line coach, the well-proportioned 10T10. Sunday family outings by bus to St Albans introduced me to 4Q4s, to whose charms I was decidedly ambivalent, especially their proliferation of small windows and pointless sloping roof line, although I was impressed by how hard and efficiently they seemed to work as they scuttled busily to and fro.

With the passage of time I came to realise that the AEC Q-type was a peculiarly London phenomenon and that it was a comparative rarity outside the capital. Indeed it was only the sales to London Transport that saved the whole concept of developing and marketing a side-engined passenger chassis from proving financially disastrous for AEC, whose sales team experienced difficulty in convincing other operators to try them out. Only 110 were produced for provincial and overseas use (including five fitted out as trolleybuses) during the almost five years that the model was offered for sale.

A quite substantial price premium was a feature which mitigated against the Q with most operators right from the start, as well as a reluctance — which London Transport did not initially share — to try out unconventional technology. But it was its mechanical and operational shortcomings such as overheating, poor manoeuvrability and unpredictable roadholding with a propensity to skid which turned even London Transport against it in the end, forcing the latter to abandon its earlier intention of relying on the Q as the standard full-sized single decker through its entire fleet and to pursue another line of innovation which led eventually to the splendid underfloor-engined TF class. But that is another story.

This history of London Transport's Qs was originally written as part of a project which also embraced all the other small bus and coach classes purchased for service in London before the war, but because of the amount of material available an editorial decision was made to produce it as a stand-alone subject. This called for the inclusion of rather more comprehensive detail on routes than I had provided and I am grateful to Malcolm Papes and the London Historical Research Group of the Omnibus Society for permission to reproduce, as an appendix, a paper which they produced on this subject some years ago.

As with most books about a period 70-plus years ago, we have had to use some photos that are of poor quality in the absence of alternatives. These have been reproduced at single column width.

As always, I would like to express my grateful thanks to all the many people who have helped me over the years by supplying information or photographs which have proved invaluable in completing this volume. Special thanks go once again to Alan Nightingale who has willingly given me access to his extensive photographic collection, the images from which help to bring the story to life. Friends from the past who have contributed posthumously with information or photographs have included the late John Aldridge, Peter Aldridge, Frank Davis, John Gillham, Ken Glazier, Les Hampton, Don Jones, Vic Jones, Ron Lunn, Prince Marshall, George Robbins, Allen T Smith, Don Thompson and Reg Westgate. Those still with us are Laurie Akehurst, Tony Beard, Alan Cross, Dave Jones, Hugh Taylor, Mick Webber and Jim Whiting. A big Thank You to you all.

KEN BLACKER
Lowestoft, November 2021

Q 1

The year 1932 marked the last full year of existence of the powerful London General Omnibus Company, and it was also the year in which the Associated Equipment Company (AEC) produced a new model, its Q-type, which represented a radically different approach to vehicle design from anything that was on the market at the time. The two companies were linked through common ownership by the Underground Electric Railways Company of London and traditionally worked closely together, so it was perhaps inevitable that the first Q-type bus, which was completed in April 1932, would join the LGOC fleet as its Q 1 which it officially did later in the same year.

The background to the design and development of the Q-type has already been extensively written about elsewhere. It suffices to record here that it was the brainchild of AEC's Chief Engineer, G J Rackham, who was responsible for its design and construction and who took great personal pride in the model even though it eventually failed to match the degree of operator acceptance and commercial success originally expected of it. The novel feature of the design was that the engine and radiator were relocated from their traditional place at the front of the chassis to a vertical position on the offside just behind the front wheel. By this means the front of the vehicle to the left of the driver could be brought into use, either to provide additional seating capacity or, with the front axle set back, to permit an entrance door to be placed right at the front within immediate view of the driver. Either way, the traditional half-cab layout could be done away with, allowing the frontal appearance of the body to be enhanced and, if required, streamlined.

The sizeable, lifelike-looking wooden model produced by AEC's experimental department during the winter of 1931/32 was intended as a guide to show the coachbuilder the modern, well-rounded style of bodywork with which the prototype was to be fitted. Although it was painted in a basic red livery and carried the GENERAL fleet name, the overall styling of white central band and black roof did not resemble current LGOC practice, and nor did the light coloured wheels. *AEC*

Rackham's design placed the engine vertically outside the chassis frame on the offside, a few feet behind the front axle, with the radiator ahead of it, the position of the latter denoted by a vertical series of air-intake slots in the offside panelling. A wire mesh grille was also provided in front of the exhaust manifold to provide further cooling. The driveline from the engine ran outside the chassis frame almost to the back axle, which was located well to the rear, largely for weight distribution purposes. Before reaching the back axle the drive shaft passed under the chassis frame – which rose at this point to clear the rear axle – to reach the worm drive differential located just inside the frame. The frame itself, as well as rising to clear the axle, was splayed outwards at this point to allow the differential to be located close to the offside, enabling the drive line to be as straight as possible. This in turn meant that there was only sufficient space outside the frame for a single rear wheel instead of the usual arrangement of two wheels side by side, a feature which could have led to deterioration in road-holding ability under certain passenger loading and road surface conditions, a risk which Rackham was presumably prepared to tolerate. The use of single wheels at the rear necessitated the fitting of larger tyres than was usual on British single deckers, 10.50 x 20, and the same were also specified at the front.

The engine installed in prototype chassis 762001 was AEC's standard 110 x 130mm petrol unit which, after several modifications to suit it to the revised environment, was classified as type A167. As fitted, it was tilted to the offside to reduce encroachment into the seating space, and it had to be built with certain main components such as inlet and exhaust manifolds, dynamo and starter all on the right for accessibility. An unusual feature was that the direction of rotation was reversed to anti-clockwise when viewed from the front, seemingly to allow torque reaction to be more easily accommodated. To minimise noise and vibration within the passenger saloon the engine was – unusually for the time – rubber mounted. The latest system of Lockheed hydraulic braking was used, and a conventional clutch and crash gearbox were fitted. The rear axle was a new design with fully floating shafts and the axle ratio was 5.2:1. Its positioning right at the back of the chassis created an unusually long wheelbase of 18ft 6ins which threatened to restrict manoeuvrability, especially when negotiating tight corners.

Although AEC did not itself build bodies, Rackham was keen to influence the style of bodywork used on the Q-types, both single and double deckers, to ensure that all would conform to a uniform, modern pattern. Under his guidance designs were produced and registered, and wooden

The completed vehicle, minus fleet names and other insignia, stands in the grounds of Chiswick Works in April 1932. Although all the main features of the original design have been incorporated, the harmonious lines shown on the wooden model have not been fully recaptured. The somewhat shallower roofline and the drastic repositioning of the headlights end up giving the vehicle something of a 'bath tub on wheels' appearance.

samples of both types were produced at Southall to about one-tenth scale, both being painted in red bearing the GENERAL fleet name. It was arranged that the LGOC would construct the bodywork for the single decker in its coachbuilding shop at Chiswick, albeit with advice from and under the surveillance of staff from AEC's drawing office. The coachworks at Chiswick existed primarily to provide bodies for the LGOC and its associated companies but they also regularly took orders from outside customers for both bus and lorry bodies as a means of keeping the works busy at what would otherwise be slack periods, and AEC was an obvious customer in view of their shared ownership.

Q 1's chassis was delivered to Chiswick on 5th May 1932 and, after making final adjustments, the new body which had been under construction in advance of its arrival, was mounted on to it on the 12th. It was apparent that the Chiswick coachbuilders had followed fairly closely the lines of Rackham's wooden model, the only notable difference being that the headlights were placed much higher than on the model, which spoilt the frontal symmetry to some extent. With its extra-long wheelbase and back wheels close up to the rear corners, fully-fronted bodywork, rounded corners to all windows, and well-curved front and rear ends, the vehicle undoubtedly looked startlingly unusual. Its colour scheme followed that of the wooden model, being in LGOC red relieved by a single off-white band below the windows, and a black roof which swept down at the rear as far as the waistrail.

The vehicle was fitted out originally as a 38-seater, a highly creditable achievement within a length of only 27ft 6ins. Initially devoid of any signwriting, it underwent a series of tests at both Southall and Chiswick. With the intention of adding it to the permanent LGOC fleet a number of

Q 1 licensed and ready for action in September 1932. Modifications to the bodywork prior to its entry into service have resulted in the fitment of prominent destination screens and roof ventilators at front and rear plus glass rainshields, while the driver now has his own entry door on the offside. The front bumper bar incorporating a registration plate is a fussy new addition, and alterations have been made to the engine cooling arrangements. *London Transport Museum*

alterations were then made to the bodywork. The front destination box was rebuilt to the standard size employed by the LGOC for its single deckers, and a similar one was added at the rear. Roof ventilators were fitted back and front, and glass louvres were mounted above all the windows to act as rain shields. The front windscreens were revised and fitted with sliding, pneumatically-controlled wipers on both windows in place of the small, conventional style wiper first fitted to the driver's screen only. As originally constructed, the vehicle had no offside driver's door and he was expected to gain access to the cab through the passenger saloon. An offside door to the cab was now provided, the window of which, along with the fixed window in front of it, was given an unusual inward tilt, the reason for which is not immediately obvious. An internal modification was the provision of a screen behind the driver where there had not been one previously.

Internally, the body was fitted out and decorated very much in accordance with standard LGOC practice at the time, making extensive use of rexine to cover all the panels and window surrounds, and using the latest type of rather spartan wooden-framed seat introduced with the 'Bluebird' LTs, the cushions and squabs of which were covered in the 'lozenge' design of moquette upon which the LGOC was standardising at the time. The unusual features about it were the windows and the doors. The former were of the full-drop variety which, though still commonly specified for luxury coach bodies, had almost disappeared from the service bus scene in favour of half-drops. The sliding entrance door, which was situated a little way back from the front axle, was manually operated. The emergency exit door was situated at the back of the vehicle where it incorporated the single rear window. This may have been seen at the time as a trendy styling feature but it meant that the door

The destination box has the same decorative outward swoop at the bottom as the LGOC employed when building its later LT class single deckers, while the black reverse curve painted on to the bodywork at the back of the rear mudguard is a fashionable feature of the time. The unusually wide emergency exit door is clearly seen in this view and can be seen in the open position overleaf. *London Transport Museum*

was unnecessarily wide (wider, in fact, than the rear destination box) and heavy, features which would have impacted unfavourably on the integral strength of the back end of the body.

After its bodywork was modified at Chiswick to suit the LGOC's requirements, Q 1 continued to undergo extensive testing and also paid a number of visits to the Public Carriage Office of the Metropolitan Police to obtain permission for its operation on public service. Records no longer exist of the dialogue between the LGOC and the police authorities, but the latter, who were notably conservative in their outlook, would undoubtedly have been surprised that the LGOC should be submitting a bus for operation within the Metropolitan Police District fitted with doors to the driver's compartment and the passenger saloon, features for which they did not normally grant permission. It was almost certainly at the police's insistence that a light bumper assembly incorporating the registration plate was added at

the front, and that the seating was reduced by one, to 37, to improve circulation space in the vicinity of the doorway.

Q 1 was formally taken into LGOC stock on 24th August 1932, registered GX 5395 and allocated body number 13466. At the time it was regarded as the joint property of AEC and the LGOC, and it was not until 1st January 1933 that the latter assumed sole ownership. Its cost at the time was shown as exactly £1,000 for the chassis and £400 for the body, but these figures were exclusive of development costs estimated as having been in the region of £1,435.

The new vehicle was allocated to Hammersmith garage on 2nd September in readiness for a much-publicised entry into service on Monday the 5th on route 11E between Liverpool Street and Shepherds Bush. The reason for selecting one of London's busiest and best-known services for its inauguration can only have been that it was a calculated attempt by the LGOC to attract

The seating arrangements for 37 can be seen in these two photos. A wonderful view of the road ahead would be obtained from the seat right at the front on the left of the driver. As well as an inward facing seat for five on the offside over the engine, a similar seat for two is positioned ahead of the entrance door to cover the front wheelarch. The three rows of seats at the back are on a raised plinth, and the comparative narrowness of the gangway emphasises the excessive width of the emergency door. The overall décor of grey and cream is relieved by a floral covering to the panels below the windows. *London Transport Museum*

Signs of bunching in Victoria Street! A largely empty LT on route 11 has caught up with Q 1 as passengers embark on a journey bound for Liverpool Street. The photograph was probably taken during one of its first days in service when such an unusual vehicle would have been universally viewed as a complete novelty, especially on a busy route serving the commercial heart of London. *London Transport Museum*

maximum publicity, since the vehicle was totally unsuited for such busy, front-line work. Its seating capacity was grossly inferior to that of the LT double deckers normally employed on the 11 group and would have proved totally inadequate, especially at peak times, while the comparative narrowness of the doorway would have made it hard for crews to keep to schedule. It was probably intended right from the start that its stay on the 11E would be short lived and it almost certainly came as no surprise when, on 28th October, it headed into the southern suburbs and Nunhead garage for operation on Peckham circular routes 621A and 621B. Even here its operation appears to have been spasmodic judging by a report from

the Omnibus Society in May 1933 stating that "Additional drivers at Nunhead are being trained in handling the vehicle, which will then resume normal operation on route 621".

Q 1 was still operating from Nunhead on 1st July 1933 when the London Passenger Transport Board took over from the LGOC, with details of its performance in comparison with conventional single deckers being carefully noted. Included amongst these observations was a study of the passenger receipts compared with those on the LT single deckers normally used on the 621 group, which proved inconclusive. Not long into the LPTB era, on 25th August 1933, Q 1 went into Chiswick Works for its first overhaul, from which it officially

Q 1 stops to take on board a full load outside the Royal Arsenal Co-op in Rye Lane, Peckham during the final days of the London General Omnibus Company when the vehicle was at work on route 621. Passengers can be seen packed uncomfortably, shoulder to shoulder, on the seat over the engine. *J F Higham © A B Cross*

emerged on 8th September. Whether or not it returned to Nunhead after overhaul is uncertain, but on 4th December 1933 it was sent to Reigate and placed on loan to the Country Bus & Coach department. It was now in Green Line colours of green and black with silver roof, and may have been painted this way at overhaul. Once again it was destined for work to which it was ill suited. Despite its very basic seating and lack of luggage racks, Q 1 was placed into service on the Redhill to

Watford section of Green Line service I. In its early days, the Country Bus & Coach department did not follow the Central Bus system of displaying garage and running number stencils so the holders for these, which had been mounted on specially-shaped bases attached to the arched centre panels of Q 1, were removed.

It is not known how long Q 1 remained on Green Line work, but its stay was probably quite brief. Apart from its bodywork shortcomings,

Q 1 in its early Country Bus days while working local circular service 427 from Reigate garage. The department's original livery combining a rather sombre green with black relief and silver roof does nothing to enhance the looks of Q 1 which is now bereft of a fleet name to break up the pugnacious appearance of its main front panel where the chromium plated headlamp surrounds have now been painted black. An additional set of sloping ventilator grilles just behind the front wheels signifies a further attempt to improve engine cooling. *George Robbins collection © A B Cross*

Seen on 24th April 1937, just a few days after emerging from its third overhaul, Q 1 now exhibits a modified front profile with the headlamps lowered to approximately the position envisaged by AEC on their original wooden model. The two-tone green livery presents a more cheerful appearance than the earlier green and black, and the garage stencil and running number plates can just be seen behind the glass in the first passenger window. *D W K Jones*

which were sure to have made it unpopular with travellers paying premium fares, it probably proved too slow for this type of work. At 5 tons 8cwt unladen it was not a particularly heavy vehicle, but under full loads its 6.12 litre engine would certainly have struggled. Interestingly, at a later but unknown date in its career, this shortcoming was acknowledged and a more powerful 7.4 litre 110 x 130 mm A169 unit was fitted instead.

After coming off Green Line service, Q1 remained at Reigate on that garage's bus service roster, and on 13th February 1934 it was officially transferred into Country Bus stock. The introduction of Central Bus-style running plates into the Country area in late 1934 did not result

in holders being restored to Q1's external panels and, instead, new stencil holders were mounted inside the body showing outwards through the windows. The 1935 introduction of the coding system to the country fleet saw Q 1 classified as 1Q1, and the Chiswick process of allocating body numbers to Country Bus vehicles upon overhaul found Q 1 receiving the new body number 15914 in September 1935.

Reigate remained Q 1's base for the remainder of its operating career with London Transport, but changes to its external appearance took place from time to time to add to its interest. It emerged from a 5½-week overhaul at Chiswick on 10th September 1935 with the front modified

Q 1's fourth overhaul occupied six weeks in August and September 1938 and produced in this remarkable transformation which resulted in the revised frontal appearance closely resembling the 4Q4 class whilst leaving the bodywork virtually unchanged from the front wheels rearwards. Q 1 is seen outside Reigate garage, possibly before the vehicle re-entered service in its revised form. *G J Robbins collection © A B Cross*

by mounting the headlights much lower down than previously, and with a fog light added. It also carried the latest country area livery consisting of two shades of green, still with a silver roof. Much more extensive overhaul work carried out between 9th August and 23rd September 1938 saw a far greater transformation. The entire front end was totally refigured ahead of the front axle to resemble the 102-strong 4Q4 fleet now in country service, thereby considerably modernising its appearance, and it now wore the new Lincoln green base colour for the first time. Internal rebuilding took place too, with the installation of a full width front bulkhead eliminating the passenger seats to the left of the driver and reducing capacity by two to 35. Unladen weight rose by 2cwt to 5tons 10cwt.

Unlike some other experimental vehicles and general oddities, Q 1 was not withdrawn from service early in the war but continued to operate normally at Reigate throughout the early years of the conflict. It was even overhauled twice during the war, in June 1940 and again in May 1942, which found it carrying the standard wartime green and white bus livery, initially with grey roof and later brown. The operational end for Q 1 finally came on 30th September 1942 when it was delicensed, subsequently spending the remaining war years in storage, firstly in Tunbridge Wells garage and later at Guildford.

Q 1 was one of a batch of four obsolete buses which were the first to be sold to dealers after the war, the other three being TF 1 and a pair of 1/7T7/1 former Green Line coaches with non-standard diesel engines, T 274 and T 305. Formal approval for their sale was given on 17th January 1946 and they left the fleet on the 23rd of the same month. Given the dire shortage of serviceable buses so soon after the war, even oddities such as Q 1 could quickly find a new niche, which in this case was with C J Towler of Emneth, in whose fleet it had appeared by March 1946. After serving Wisbech and the towns and villages on the Norfolk/Cambridgeshire border for five years, the prototype Q finally came to the end of the road in March 1951. It remained in Emneth to end its days as a chicken house.

Its days are numbered and a forlorn looking Q 1 silently awaits its inevitable fate. Under Towler's ownership the indicator box was removed, and though this would have eased the strain on the rear of the bodywork, it was clearly not enough to keep the wide and heavy emergency door hanging straight on its hinges. *Alan B Cross*

Although its bodywork was built at Chiswick and followed closely the lines of the wooden model of a double deck Q provided by AEC, the prototype did not carry GENERAL livery as the model had done and, as far as is known, never operated in London. This front view shows clearly the lightweight bumper-cum-lifeguard arrangement recommended by AEC.

THE DOUBLE DECKERS: Q 2 – Q 5

AEC had always intended to develop a double deck version of the Q and construction of the first prototype had almost been completed by the time Q 1 entered service on route 11E. As in the case of Q 1, the contract for construction of the body was placed with the LGOC, and one of the first outings away from Southall for the prototype chassis 761001 took it to Chiswick where it stayed between 27th September and 5th October 1932 while the body was installed and fitted out. The vehicle was subsequently taxed for road use in January 1933 as AHX 63 but, unlike its single deck counterpart, did not carry the GENERAL fleet name and was never trialled in service by the LGOC.

It is interesting to recall that the body of AHX 63 was one of two double deckers constructed at Chiswick for the LGOC at that time, both carrying the innovative and ultra-modern outline designed by Rackham and his team at AEC. The other was placed on experimental trolleybus chassis 691T001, and although this was a three-axle centre-entrance vehicle, the similarities between the two were very clear both externally and, more particularly in regard to their interior finish where features such as ceiling design, seats, and the preference for rexine over polished wood were all typical of Chiswick-built bodies. Although AHX 63 was spurned by the LGOC, the trolleybus, registered AHX 801, found almost instant use on loan to associated company London United Tramways with whom it entered experimental service on 27th March 1933, being subsequently purchased by London Transport and numbered 61 in March 1934.

AEC pinned great faith on the double deck Q and was initially hopeful that it would interest the LGOC sufficiently to place large orders for it. The Q's big selling point was that it offered the opportunity to squeeze as many as 60 seats comfortably within its 26ft length – in fact the prototype originally seated 62 but two of these were quickly removed from the upper deck, possibly because they were found to infringe the legal laden weight limit. Unlike its single deck equivalent, the double deck Q was designed so that passengers boarded at the very front, next to the driver, for which purpose the front axle was located further back with a consequent reduction in wheelbase length. In abandoning the traditional rear platform the Q double decker was years ahead of its time, and it was not until the Leyland Atlantean gained acceptance more than 20 years later that this concept finally took hold.

It must have come as a big disappointment to AEC to find that the LGOC did not immediately toy with the idea of placing an order for Q-type double deckers. The model's unconventional entrance and seating layout may have served as a big deterrent but is also likely that the lack of an oil-engined version clouded the LGOC's judgement. However an LGOC associate company, London General Country Services, showed its willingness to experiment with a pair of double deck Qs even though these would be petrol-engined. Somewhat perversely, however, it was not interested in exploiting the ability to incorporate an entrance at the front ahead of the wheels but was keen on the centre entrance layout demonstrated on trolleybus AHX 801 to which the chassis layout was well suited provided that, as with the trolleybus, the nearside chassis framework was modified to accommodate the entrance step. This meant cranking the nearside chassis member downwards to give a low step height and also repositioning and amending the shape of the petrol tank.

Discussions took place with AEC during the first half of 1933 and quotations and possible delivery dates were established.

This process was still ongoing when the London Passenger Transport Board came into existence on 1st July 1933, and it was under the aegis of

The unusual one-piece rear emergency window with sloping sides, which also featured on the trolleybus body built at the same time, was subsequently adopted by London Transport as a standard fitting for its massive fleet of new trolleybuses built from 1935 onwards.

the new organisation that a contract for the two vehicles at £1,903 apiece was placed through a Special Requisition Order of 17th July which also included 12 low-height, front entrance oil-engined AEC Regents, also for Country area use, at a cost of £1,725 each. The difference in price between the two models is indicative of the high cost of the Q type compared with a conventional vehicle. Even though the Regents would have benefited from some level of quantity discount to reduce their basic price, this would probably have been more than balanced by the higher cost of their oil engines, leaving a differential of some 11% between the two.

BPG 507 was the second double deck Q built by AEC with chassis frame modified to accommodate a centre entrance, the first having been demonstrated at the 1933 Olympia show and subsequently sold to Grimsby Corporation. Photographed at the AEC works when brand new with doors open to show the entrance step and staircase layout, it displays GREEN LINE insignia as well as the recently-adopted LONDON TRANSPORT fleet name. It also carries the front bumper and tram-like lifeguard, both of which may have been removed before it entered service. *London Transport Museum*

The driver's cab on BPJ 224 was a compact affair. The positioning of the handbrake lever and the bulb horn made it a little tortuous to climb into, but at least the driver had the benefit of a full height hinged door to cut out draughts. *London Transport Museum*

This was, in fact, the first order ever placed by London Transport for new double deckers. LGCS had not used fleet numbers for its buses, referring to them only by their registration numbers, and this system was perpetuated by the new Country Bus & Coach department of the LPTB in its early days. The registration numbers subsequently allocated to the two new Qs were BPG 507 and BPJ 224 and this is how they were officially referred to until the big reorganisation of 25th February 1935 when the Chiswick-based system of vehicle control became all-embracing and they were then numbered Q 4 and Q 5.

London General Country Services had been a renaming of the former East Surrey Traction Company which, in its latter days, had built up a close working relationship with the Weymann coachbuilding concern whose factory was located within its operating territory at Addlestone. Back

BPJ 224 poses for the official photographer prior to entering service at Reigate, now replete with destination blinds but minus the GREEN LINE fleet names and without any front bumper gear fitted. As an embellishment, its tyres have been painted white in stark contrast to the black wheel rims, orange wheel centres and chromium plated wheel rings. At this stage the legal address of the Country Bus department is still shown as Bell Street, Reigate, but this will be changed to 55 Broadway with the reorganisation of February 1935. *London Transport Museum*

Taken on the same occasion, this view shows the largely upright rear profile of BPJ 224 and the standard London Transport emergency window with its Y-shaped central pillar. The light-coloured panel covering the inside of the staircase window looks somewhat incongruous against the green and black bodywork. Operating experience has resulted in the fitment of a much larger wire mesh panel alongside the engine exhaust than was used on Q 1. *London Transport Museum*

in 1931 it had ordered nine new single deckers – 3 AEC Regals and 6 Morris Commercial Viceroys – with Weymann bodywork to its own specification, which bore very little similarity to then-current LGOC practice. The same now applied to the two double deck Qs and to the twelve low-height

Regents which Weymann was also contracted to supply, both groups of vehicle being based on MCW-type metal framework and bearing little physical similarity – apart from their three-piece front and rear destinations screens and Y-style emergency exits – to then-current Chiswick practice.

EMERGENCY EXIT

SURBITON
TOLWORTH
EWELL

406

KINGSTON S^{TN}

EMERGENCY EXIT LIFT TO OPEN

3647 N

BPJ
224

The first tentative connection that the Central Bus department had with the double deck Q came four weeks after the formation of London Transport when, at a meeting at 55 Broadway of the Traffic Committee, Frank Pick himself proposed obtaining two of them for experimental operation on outer suburban services. Unlike the LGCS pair, these would be of AEC's standard front-entrance type with open doorway ahead of the front axle. The proposal was immediately adopted, and no time was lost in despatching observers to Birmingham and Liverpool to report on the operations of the first two double deck Qs to be produced. Both of these were originally built as demonstrators but were subsequently taken permanently into the fleets of Birmingham City Transport (who purchased the original prototype AHX 63) and Crosville Motor Services respectively. AEC had concluded an arrangement with Metro Cammell to construct bodies at its Saltley works for early production Q double deckers based on its own registered design and incorporating MCW-patented steel framework. London Transport's order, which was authorised on 2nd October, specified bodywork from this manufacturer, and fleet numbers Q2 and Q3 were allocated to the new vehicles along with registration numbers AYV 615/616.

Events were moving very quickly and it was anticipated that the chassis for all four Qs would be completed before the end of the year. Meanwhile detailed drawings of the proposed bodywork for Q2 and Q3 were approved on 21st August 1933, and it was decided that they would be painted in an appropriately modified STL style livery of red with white (officially grey) window frames and silver roof rather than in the style applied to AEC's wooden model, and that they would be 59-seaters.

The four chassis finally produced in response to the two orders were 761011 and 761012 for Q 2 and Q 3 respectively, 761104 for BPG 507 and 761107 for BPJ 224. The chassis of Q 2 was received, and no doubt closely examined, at Chiswick on 21st November 1933, but the others probably all went straight from Southall to their respective coachbuilders. All four were petrol engined with A169 110mm x 130mm 7.4 litre units but they

differed from Q 1, as did all subsequently-built Q chassis for all operators, in having fluid flywheel transmissions and vacuum operated preselector gearboxes. The crash gearbox on Q 1 had proved problematical to drivers, mainly because it was situated behind them and not within easy earshot, leading AEC to delete it from all future options. All four double deckers had a 15ft 0ins wheelbase chassis with standard vacuum hydraulic braking, large 11.25 x 20 tyres all round, and 6⅕:1 rear axle ratio. Whilst all four were fitted with fluid flywheels manufactured at Southall under Daimler licence, Qs 2 and 3 had Daimler-built preselector gearboxes while the two country area vehicles were equipped with preselect boxes built by AEC under licence from Improved Cars Ltd. The latter had drives and bands of increased size, as was the top speed cone, but because of differences in selector control mechanism and in their mounting arrangements the two types were not interchangeable. Coincidentally (and rather improbably) when bodies were fitted, all four vehicles were shown as having exactly the same unladen weight of 6tons 4cwt 2qrs despite the big differences in specification between the Central area vehicles and the country ones.

It is not known for certain which of the four arrived at Chiswick first in completed form. BPG 507 is known to have been taken on books on 18th May 1934 and Q 3 on 25th May, but dates for the other two have not been recorded. It is certainly probable that all four were in stock by the end of May. None were immediately placed into service, and it was eventually the two red ones that were allocated to a garage first, Q 2 on 5th July 1934 and Q 3 the next day at Harrow Weald, from which they entered service on 23rd July on suburban route 114 between Mill Hill and South Harrow.

Metro Cammell's bodies for these two followed almost exactly AEC's design guidelines which included a curved, modernistic front end, wide windows with rounded corners, and three prominent moulded sections of panel, one beneath the windows on each deck and a third around the centre of the vehicle. The wide platform, for which no doors were provided, was placed ahead of the front axle giving direct access to the driver

with the staircase immediately behind him. For a reason that has not been recorded, the seating capacity was subsequently reduced at London Transport's request to 56 (28 on each deck), somewhat nullifying one of the main benefits of the design concept. The only glaringly obvious special features were the provision of London Transport's standard triple indicator box layout front and rear and its own style of rear emergency window with Y-shaped centre pillar. Internally, the extensive use of rexine to cover almost all panels and mouldings, a styling feature inherited from the LGOC, was perpetuated, and the seats were the same type of wooden-framed units as had been used on Q 1 but covered in a patterned green moquette.

When posed for the photographer at Chiswick, Q 2 was fitted out to work from Chalk Farm garage on route 77, on which it never ran. Some aspects of the body design, and especially the frontal treatment, appear more neatly finished than on the Country Bus Qs, but Qs 2 and 3 lacked the opening front windows and between-decks ventilation grilles of their country counterparts and their one-piece lower body side panels would have made damage repair less easy. The platform step arrangement can be clearly seen through the open doorway with stairs ascending to the upper deck immediately behind the driver, all forming a pinchpoint which proved detrimental at busy times. At the back end, which was not quite so starkly upright as on the country area pair, the emergency window was set into the back dome at a much higher level than usual, well above the height of the front and side windows. Unlike the country Qs, the silver roof extends to cover the rear dome where it drops down at the corners as far as the foot of the windows. *London Transport Museum*

Looking towards the rear in the lower saloons of Q 2 and BPJ 224, the stark difference in approach between the design teams at Chiswick and Reigate in relation to internal fitments and décor is immediately obvious. Whether related to the comfort and appearance of the seats (low backed and basic or higher backed with attractive coverings), the light fittings (starkly utilitarian plain bulbs or ornamental jellymould lamp covers), or the general décor (plain grey rexine or polished mahogany), the differences between the two could hardly be greater. The Country Bus vehicle has the drawback of more inward-facing seats but offers a splendid view of the road ahead for those at the front. *London Transport Museum*

The Weymann bodies on the two Country area buses followed the same standard AEC outline with prominently curved front and largely upright rear, but instead of the open doorway ahead of the front axle, the entry point was almost in the centre and was enclosed by a pair of driver-controlled pneumatically-operated sliding doors supplied by G D Peters, with the spiral-type staircase facing them. In contrast to Q 2 and Q 3 the driver had his own hinged access door on the offside of the vehicle. The repositioning of the passenger doorway resulted in a revised pillar spacing and the insertion of an extra bay, which meant that the six extra-wide windows on the upper sides of the standard AEC design were replaced by seven shorter ones. The same London Transport indicator box and emergency window arrangement as applied to Qs 2 and 3 were used here too, but a notable omission was the convex central waist panel. A photograph of BPG 507 when new shows that it was originally equipped with a front bumper arrangement as used on most provincial double deck Qs, consisting of a lightweight bar which, when struck, tripped a tramcar-type lifeguard mounted just in front of the

wheels, but this was removed before the vehicle entered service and it is not known whether the same devices were originally fitted to the other three or if this was a one-off.

Internally the Reigate-specified décor resulted in a far more sumptuous appearance than on Qs 2 and 3, with extensive use of polished mahogany mouldings and the provision of attractive, curved-back metal-framed seats upholstered in very attractive, large patterned moquette. This same eye-catching styling was also present on the twelve Regents ordered at the same time which subsequently became STL 1044-1055 in the London Transport fleet. The seating layout was obviously completely different from that on the Central area buses, and while the lower deck achieved the same capacity of 28 seats the upper saloon accommodated one fewer at 27. The two vehicles were painted externally in the then-standard country livery of green and black with silver roof.

The two green Qs originally carried GREEN LINE fleet names as well as LONDON TRANSPORT, but there is no evidence that they ever operated on Green Line service and the names were

BPJ 224 again. It can be seen that the stairwell was made as unobtrusive as possible and an earlier photograph shows that, as originally built, a single seat was provided at the head of the stairs adjacent to the case containing the nearside route blind. Presumably as an aid to manoeuvrability, it had been removed by the time these photographs were taken, reducing the upper deck seating capacity to 27. Note that, in order to enhance the general air of ornateness and opulence, even the floor lino is patterned. The back window design, which remained specific to London, incorporates a red knob in the centre of the inverted triangle which is pressed to release the window in an emergency. *London Transport Museum*

quickly removed. Both vehicles were despatched to Leatherhead garage during the first week of August 1934 where they became a regular feature for almost four years on routes 406 (Kingston to Redhill) and 408 (West Croydon to Guildford). As in the case of single deck Q 1, holders for garage stencils and running numbers were fixed to them towards the end of 1934, and once the country fleet had been absorbed into the Chiswick system they were allocated fleet numbers Q 4 (BPG 507) and Q 5 (BPJ 224) Body numbers 16086 and 16593 were issued to Q 4 and Q 5 as they passed through overhaul in November 1935 and April 1936 respectively, at which time they received the new standard Country Bus dual-green livery. Under the fleet classification system they became class 3Q3, the two Central Bus vehicles having been coded 2Q2.

In the Central area the two Qs remained on outer suburban operation during their initial running-in period, but a scheme was quickly hatched to test them on a busier, in-town service in due course. Their stint at Harrow Weald garage on route 114 lasted from July 1934 through to the end of that year. On 2nd January 1935 they moved to Middle Row garage to take up residence on route 52, which found them still setting out from Mill Hill but now running southwards from there into the heart of London to terminate at Victoria Station. Official fears that the positioning of the open doorway ahead of the front axle would provoke an increase in boarding and alighting accidents proved unfounded, but an unexpected shortcoming that quickly came to light arose through locating the stairs immediately behind the driver where a bottleneck formed at the foot of the staircase at busy times, nullifying the effectiveness of the wide entrance platform. As early as October 1934 there was consensus for the view that a centre entrance would be a better proposition on any future Q-type double deckers purchased for Central Buses, and Chief Engineer A A M (Bill) Durrant was asked to start work on a suitable design which, as far as is known, never saw the light of day.

In December 1934 and January 1935 respectively Q 2 and Q 3 were both reduced to 55-seaters through the removal of a seat from the upper deck, presumably at the top of the staircase to improve circulation there. This meant that both vehicles, which were designed by AEC to be 60-seaters, now carried fewer passengers than the standard STL. A few months later A C Richardson, the Operating Manager for Central Buses, suggested that the two Qs should be subjected to more intense testing by transferring them to a route serving the City of London and carrying a higher proportion of short distance travellers than the 52. This idea was vetoed by Frank Pick, and it appears that the department's interest in the two vehicles faded away thereafter. By 1937 it had been decided that they could be more appropriately employed by working alongside Qs 4 and 5 on country service and an arrangement was made to send them to the Country Bus & Coach department in exchange for ST 818 and ST 819. On 24th May 1937 Qs 2 and 3 both went to Chiswick for what must have been a very cursory overhaul from which they emerged in green livery a few days later, their official allocation date to Leatherhead being 29th May.

In 1938 the operation of double deck Qs from Leatherhead came to an end, and between 23rd June and 12th July Q 2-5 made their way to Hertford to provide an updating of this garage's trunk service 310 (Hertford-Enfield) in place of its usual STs. After almost exactly a year at Hertford, all four were on the move again between 1st July and 1st August 1939. Before this, however, they had all received their third overhaul between April and July 1939 which resulted in them appearing for the first time in the new, darker Lincoln green shade of paint now standard for the country fleet. Furthermore, two of them, Q 2 and Q 5, had adopted a revised frontal appearance thanks to the attachment of a somewhat rudimentary outline of an AEC radiator below the windscreens, which could hardly have fooled anyone into thinking that it was the real thing. This marked the resumption of a supposed problem first encountered in 1936 when it had been suggested that, because the Q-type had no radiator at the front, confusion was caused through difficulty in knowing which way the bus was going!

Q 2 and Q 3 stayed barely six months at Harrow Weald, but long enough for them to run-in and expose any basic faults. Q 3 is seen in its early days on route 114 and later, when working from Middle Row, at Victoria station on the far busier 52. On both occasions the route number blinds displayed old-style numerals from the LGOC days. In the later photograph the driver's mirror has been re-sited to a lower position, presumably as an outcome of service experience, and a nearside one has been added at cantrail level. More noticeably from a passenger's viewpoint, it has now acquired opening front windows. *J F Higham © A B Cross*

Even though the staircase and the seating layouts differed considerably from the standard London pattern, the general appearance of the interior on Qs 2 and 3 would have seemed very familiar to regular passengers accustomed to travelling on contemporary STLs. The only hint of non-LPTB décor was a single polished moulding running the length of both decks above the windows. The unusually high positioning of the emergency window is immediately apparent in the upper deck view.
London Transport Museum

The final garage to which the four vehicles moved was Grays where they arrived between 1st July and 1st August 1939, but it has not been established what route(s) they ran on there. Shortly before arriving at Grays the two centre entrance vehicles were reduced to 53 seaters through the removal of the pair of seats at the very front of the lower saloon adjacent to the driver. Although it could not have been foreseen at the time, their service days with London Transport were soon to end as a result of the outbreak of war. On 30th September 1939 all four were delicensed as a result of the early wartime service reductions, and they were destined never to run in service for London Transport again.

Prohibited under wartime restrictions from selling redundant vehicles, London Transport was obliged to keep the four double deck Qs in storage if no other use could be found for them. In 1941, and again in 1943, all four served occasional spells as local Home Guard headquarters at garages such as Godstone, East Grinstead, Swanley, Hertford and Watford High Street, and it was while serving in this capacity at Swanley that Q 3 was destroyed by enemy action and was officially written off books

Above The two green double deck Qs spent almost four years at Leatherhead. Seen passing Kingston garage, BPJ 224 has now received its fleet number Q 5 and carries standard garage and running number plates in a holder installed on the curved body panel. This was before Q 5 went in for its first overhaul in February 1936 from which it emerged in the new two-tone green livery. *J F Higham © A B Cross*

Facing page top After being repainted green, Q 2 and Q 3 arrived at Hertford garage in June and July 1938 respectively to take up service on route 310. Q 2 is seen in the wide open spaces of Hertford bus station. *J F Higham © A B Cross*

Facing page bottom left Now running from Hertford garage post-June 1938, Q 5 is seen at the Enfield terminus of route 310 under the recently installed trolleybus overhead wiring. Structurally it is still basically in its original condition after five years of operation except that its side lights have now been moved from their original position and built much lower down into the bodywork at waistrail level. *D Evans © Omnibus Society*

Facing page bottom right Q 2 stands at the Enfield terminus soon after its third and last overhaul in May 1939 wearing the darker, Lincoln green livery. Most obvious among the alterations is the unconvincing and unflattering dummy radiator including an air inlet below the registration plate, while a fog lamp has now been added and all the convex body panels have been replaced by flat ones. *D Evans © Omnibus Society*

on 30th April 1941. One by one the other three all drifted into the well-known storage yard at Forest Road, Walthamstow (often wrongly referred to by staff as Ferry Lane) between September 1943 and August 1944, where they could be tantalisingly glimpsed from the upper deck of passing 623 and 625 trolleybuses.

The early post-war years saw a renewal of activity for the three remaining vehicles after six wartime years away from front line service, but not in London. Sold in March 1946 to Lancashire Motor Traders, they were all quickly snapped up by new owners. The former Q 2 found itself, with its top deck removed, running as a 31-seat coach until its final retirement as a mobile snack bar, but the other two both resumed a fully active life as stage carriage buses. Q4 was kept busy with one of the well-known Doncaster independents, G H Ennifer's Blue Ensign, whilst Q 5 worked with H Brown of Garelochhead in rural Argyllshire until becoming a caravan in 1950.

Q 3 is Hertford bound as it passes through Hoddesdon in a snowy scene during the winter of 1938/39. At this stage it is still in the condition in which it arrived at Hertford from Leatherhead. *Mick Webber collection*

All of the double deck Qs that survived the war found a new life with new owners in the early post-war years. The only one to be drastically altered was Q 2 which, having been cut down to a single decker with a door at the front and an emergency exit cut into the offside, served as a rather weird looking coach with Lindon's of Windle, near St. Helens, before ending its days as a snack bar last seen in Leicester in about February 1951. *J F Higham © A B Cross*

After leaving London Q 4 joined the Blue Ensign fleet of G H Ennifer Ltd, one of four operators running a frequent joint service between Doncaster and the outlying village of Rossington. These two views were taken at Doncaster's Glasgow Paddocks bus station in September 1950. The polished strips on the front dash would have been the work of Blue Ensign, but two features from its later London Transport days are in evidence and were probably installed at its final overhaul in May 1939. On the nearside, the top of the first lower deck window now slopes upwards to provide better visibility for the driver, while on the offside a route number stencil holder has been provided on the staircase panel. Q 4 ran for Blue Ensign until about January 1952 and was the last of the old London Transport double deck Qs to remain in passenger service. *Geoffrey Morant*

Still sporting its dummy AEC-style radiator, the former Q 5 saw regular passenger service from the latter half of 1946 onwards with H Brown of Garelochhead until it was sold in 1950 and ended its days as a caravan. The unflattering all-red livery is broken only by the prominent display by GENASPRIN whose adverts also featured prominently on buses in London for very many years. *Geoffrey Morant*

COUNTRY BUSES: Q 6 – Q 105, Q 186, Q 187

At a meeting of senior management on 17th July 1933, barely more than a fortnight after the LPTB had taken over, the General Manager of the new Country Bus & Coach department, A H Hawkins, broached the idea of acquiring a fleet of AEC Q-types to replace the miscellany of single deckers in the 30-seat range that his department had already acquired or anticipated doing so. He submitted drawings of a proposed 36-seater produced by Duple, who had recently been contracted by AEC to build the bodies for its initial production run of single deckers. It appears that Frank Pick, who was chairing the meeting, immediately dismissed the Duple design, taking a particular dislike to its use of sloped pillars which had presumably been included to further its appearance of modernity, and he informed his managers that they need not necessarily expect that, just because a few Qs were being purchased experimentally, further vehicles of this type would be acquired. Nevertheless, he obviously kept an open mind about the suitability or otherwise of the Q-type as he instructed A A

M Durrant, who had now been appointed as the LPTB's Chief Engineer, to examine the matter and report back.

The outcome is well known. The Board's top engineers, all inherited directly from the LGOC, had already come to the conclusion that a front-mounted engine was not the best arrangement for large capacity single deckers and, whilst preferring to have the engine placed amidships under the floor or at the very back of the vehicle, they accepted that the Q-type was the only viable alternative on the market at the time. Furthermore, it was just then becoming known that an oil-engined version of the Q was being developed, which made it far more attractive.

With all the windows fully dropped on a hot summer day in 1935, Q 6 pauses on its journey to Enfield on route 306 to pick up a lady passenger. Meanwhile two young children enjoy the view from the front seat adjacent to the driver which, in the case of Q 6, was removed in July 1936. The even window spacing makes for a more harmonious design on the nearside. *J F Higham © A B Cross*

The ingenious Q-type chassis was adopted by London Transport as the only solution available at the time in its quest to relocate the engine away from the front on single deckers to free up floor space and provide greater seating capacity. The photograph of an unidentified chassis shows the characteristic narrow frame, widening out at the rear where it rises above the differential to permit a straight transmission line but restricting the space available for the rear wheels.

The exact timescale of events which followed is not known, but certainly by the spring of 1934 arrangements were in hand to procure 100 oil-engined Q-type single deckers for the Country Bus & Coach department, specifically to replace 89 ADC416, 10 Dennis and a single Thornycroft. The Chiswick coachbuilding shops were too busy to construct the bodywork so tenders were issued to outside contractors for the supply of 100 metal-framed 38-seat bodies.

AEC would have been delighted and perhaps even a little surprised to receive such a large order. The Q had not been as popularly received as had been anticipated, and the Company had been struggling to achieve sufficient sales to make the

project worthwhile and to recoup its development costs. A contract was placed with the Birmingham Railway Carriage & Wagon Company (BRCW) of Smethwick to construct the bodies. These were fated to be the only type of bus body ever built by BRCW for London Transport, although the Company supplied 390 trolleybus bodies in six batches between 1935 and 1939. BRCW employed MCW-type metal framework in all its road vehicle bodies and became known for the high standard of its workmanship. The bodies for Q 6-105 were designed at Chiswick but incorporated a number of AEC-inspired design features, one of which was a roof line which sloped very visibly downwards from front to rear. This was a new refinement added to the AEC specification after the construction of Q 1, presumably with the aim of projecting an even more modern and aerodynamic look even though it inevitably added to the complexity and cost of construction.

The offside drawing, produced for the 'Bus & Coach' journal in 1934, depicts the neat way in which the engine and transmission are mounted outside the offside frame member, and also shows a spare wheel carrier which did not feature on London Transport's vehicles.

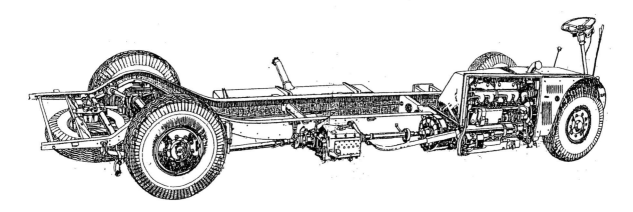

The order for what became known as the 4Q4 class was authorised on 28th August 1934 at an estimated total cost of £173,600, and the specification for the 100 bodies was finalised for despatch to BRCW on 20th September. Body numbers 14990-15089 were allocated in numerical order, and likewise registration numbers were reserved as BXD 527-576 (Q 6-55) and CGJ 161-210 (Q56-105), although for some unknown reason those on Q 19 and Q 20 were transposed to make them BXD 541 and BXD 540 respectively. Chassis numbers consisted of the block 0762057-156 but these were not issued to vehicles in any particular sequence, the earliest chassis, 0762057, being Q 17 while the last vehicle to be bodied, Q 105, carried early chassis 0762066.

In terms of external dimensions, the 4Q4s were the same as Q 1 with an overall length of 27ft 6ins and the same extra-long 18ft 6ins wheelbase. Clayton Dewandre servo-assisted Lockheed braking, preselector gearbox and fluid flywheel, AEC worm and nut steering and 10.50 x 20 low pressure tyres were all part of the specification. Unlike Q 1 the gearbox was not unit mounted with the engine but was separately located much further back, bolted on to the outside of the chassis frame and readily accessible through outward opening panels in the lower bodywork.

The first Qs in the London fleet with oil engines, the 4Q4s employed the new AEC-built A170. This used the Ricardo 'Comet' indirect injection system and, with bore and stroke dimensions of 106mm x 146mm, produced a swept volume of 7.731 litres. When subsequently widely introduced throughout the rest of the manufacturer's range in A171 form, this engine became known as the famous AEC 7.7 and remained in production for about the next 20 years. In contrast to the engines on Q 1-5, these were solid mounted so the ride was inevitably rougher, and they were also considerably noisier, but with a rear axle ratio set at 5¼ :1 the 4Q4s proved to be more than adequate for their destined role as country buses.

The bodies on the 4Q4s were strikingly modern for their time, though not particularly handsome. AEC's concept of a raked roof did little to improve the overall appearance and, if anything, looked somewhat gimmicky. London Transport opted for shorter window bays than AEC had envisaged, which gave a rather fussy appearance, especially on the offside where the emergency door was sited, but at least the error on Q 1 of trying to accommodate the single back window within an extra-wide emergency door had not been repeated. A styling feature introduced by the Chiswick design staff, and perpetuated on all subsequent single deck designs up to the start of the war, was a slight outward swoop at the bottom of the back panels which certainly helped to enhance the overall appearance. The Board's current two-tone green livery was applied with even the roof in green instead of the usual silver, black being confined to the mouldings separating the two shades of green plus the mudguards.

The 4Q4 body probably appeared at its least attractive when viewed from the back from which angle the rather pointless sloped pitch of the roofline was at its most obvious. A design feature that London Transport perpetuated on its single deckers throughout the nineteen-thirties was the outward sweep at the foot of the back panels, below which was a polished built-in bumper. Q 87 was new to Guildford on 1st November 1935 and was photographed at Merrow early in its working career. *London Transport Museum*

Inside the 4Q4, the obvious point of note was the use of modernistic pressed metal cappings around the windows in place of the usual plethora of wooden mouldings, a feature first introduced by London Transport on its initial order for Leyland Cubs and destined to be included on future new single deckers for many years to come. The standard brown and green colour scheme with cream ceiling panels dominated the interior, and the seats were of the then-standard wooden-framed variety with green moquette-covered cushions and brown and green painted backs. Largely because of the siting of the engine, the seating arrangement was a little convoluted. On the nearside a forward-facing seat for two beside the driver was placed ahead of an inward-facing seat for three, after which came the sliding door. Behind this on the nearside were six transverse

An ultra-modern feature of the BRCW-built bodies on the 4Q4s was the use of moulded window cappings made in aluminium and covered in pale green rexine at the top and brown below with polished metal bracelets separating the two colours. These photographs taken inside Q 7 show the front end layout prior to the insertion of a full-width bulkhead, while the rearward facing view shows the raised platforms on which the four rear rows of seats are situated, and the gradually diminishing ceiling height. *London Transport Museum*

seats for two, with a bench seat for five across the back. On the offside, a single bench seat for six over the engine faced inwards, and beyond it were five transverse seats for two, bringing the full total to 38, considerably in excess of all other single deckers owned by London Transport. The rearmost three rows of transverse seats and the bench at the rear were mounted higher than the remainder on a shallow plinth to minimise wheelarch intrusion. The complete vehicle officially weighed in at 5tons 12cwt unladen.

The first 4Q4 to be allocated to a garage was Q 8 at Watford High Street on 6th July 1935. This set a pattern, which was subsequently followed at most garages, of providing a vehicle for staff training ahead of the main service introduction which, in Watford High Street's case, came on the 10th. As new vehicles flooded in they were received at 16 Country area garages in the order as follows: July – Watford High Street (final total 15), Dartford (6), Amersham (4). August – Hertford (10), Hatfield (4), Leatherhead (6). September – Watford Leavesden Road (15), Swanley (5), Reigate (6), Addlestone (4), Dunton Green (2). October – Godstone (2), Dorking (4). November – Guildford (8), Windsor (8). December – St. Albans (1). The composition of the Country Bus & Coach fleet was changing dramatically at this time. In the four weeks from 8th September to 5th October, for instance, 20 new 4Q4s were taken into stock while

the departures comprised 4 Gilfords, 1 Commer, 1 Dennis, 5 AEC S-type and 14 ADC416.

Unfortunately this influx of brand new vehicles went much less well than management had anticipated, and they must have felt themselves assailed from all sides. The drivers were almost immediately up in arms, claiming that the 4Q4s were almost impossible to handle safely after dark because of reflection from the interior lighting on the windscreens which, though bad all round, was particularly intense on the nearside where it was often impossible to see the kerb. The Board's own Claims Officer, who dealt with insurance matters, was unhappy because, within a matter of weeks of their introduction into service, he had been called upon to investigate two serious instances of passengers, who were sitting on the bench seat opposite the doorway, being dislodged from their seat and falling down the steps, through the door (which had been left open) and into the roadway. To make matters even worse, by November 1935 the Metropolitan Traffic Commissioner had started expressing concern about manoeuvring difficulties with the vehicles, especially on corners, because of their front overhang and wide turning circle, and started requiring each individual route to be tested before he would allow their use. Clearly something had to be done urgently.

Early in October 1935 brand new Q 52 was commandeered by technicians from Chiswick

The relatively poor manoeuvrability of the 4Q4s, particularly when cornering in tight places, was always one of their main drawbacks and never more so than on route 425 (Dorking-Guildford) from which the Metropolitan Traffic Commissioner banned their use over certain sections of road. Guildford's Q 92 is seen on the 425 in the early days of its life but, as can be seen by the deletions on the destination blind, diversions away from the villages of Shere and Shalford have had to be made on a temporary basis until more suitable vehicles become available. *Alan B Cross*

before it could reach its nominated garage, Watford High Street, and used as a test bed for curing the windscreen reflection problems as well as trying to make the inward-facing seat over the engine safer. The latter was accepted as being a design shortcoming and it proved easier to cure than the windscreen problem. Armrests were inserted all along the seat to give passengers added stability, particularly when the vehicle was cornering, and it was generally agreed that the problem was thereby solved even though it reduced the capacity of the long seat from six to five and reduced the overall seating capacity to 37.

In the hope of tackling the windscreen reflection problem, after dark trials were tried with various types of folding canvas screens, and attempts were made to shield the foremost nearside interior lamps which were thought to be a major cause of the trouble. Nothing proved completely successful, and in the end a partition with an adjustable blind was constructed to the left of the driver with a narrow opening through which he could still, in theory, observe the front nearside corner. In this form, Q 52 was placed into service at Leatherhead on 17th October from where it went to various other garages to obtain a wide range of opinions. The result was unanimous agreement from drivers that the arrangement was not sufficiently effective and, to make matters worse, the slope of the new partition caused a severe draught in the driver's cab. The research team was forced to announce that – as they had suspected all along – the only satisfactory solution would be to install a full-width bulkhead behind the driver, which could be equipped with night blinds and would have to include a door to the cab to act as an emergency exit for the driver if needed. This would result in the loss of the two front passenger seats, meaning a further reduction in total capacity to 35.

By mid-December 1935 Q 52 had been fitted with a full-width bulkhead and was back in service. On the 20th of that month it was decided to convert the whole 4Q4 batch similarly, subject only to minor modifications to the bulkhead design, the need for which had become apparent whilst in service. The cost would amount to about £35 per bus. In addition to the seat and bulkhead modifications, it was subsequently arranged that the positioning of the side lights at the front of the vehicles should be improved. The original arrangement, which was a London Transport design speciality and had been applied to a large number of new buses and trolleybuses, placed the side lights behind small rectangular glasses located up high at cantrail level which, in the case of the 4Q4s, meant that they were placed in each corner of the front dome. These were never really effective and were superseded on the 4Q4s by larger and much more conventional lamp holders at the usual waistrail level. Also at the front, but on the very bottom panel at a level below the main headlights, two quite shapely wire mesh grilles were inserted to improve air circulation, particularly to the front brakes. It took six months to complete all this modification work on the 4Q4s, which commenced in the last week of April 1936 and was completed on 24th October.

In the meantime a decision was taken in October 1935 to place an order for two more 4Q4s with AEC and BRCW at a total coast of £1,725 each. This was coupled with an authority to order two additional Leyland Cubs, likewise to an existing design, all four vehicles being required to provide additional rolling stock needed for the summer months and to speed up the rate of overhauls in the winter. Orders for the four vehicles were placed in November 1935, and the two new 4Q4s were received in June and entered service at St Albans on 6th and 7th July 1936. A batch of 80 Qs having already been ordered for Central Bus work, these two had to be given fleet numbers following on as Q 186 and Q 187 although their chassis numbers 0762178/179 were ahead of the Central Bus batch. Registered CLE 127/128, they were allocated body numbers 16526/16527. They arrived carrying all the latest modifications, it having been necessary to reimburse BRCW for the extra cost of including these after construction had commenced.

Instead of marking a settling-in period for the 4Q4s, 1936 turned out to be anything but. Operationally, grumbles continued to come from staff about performance, notably on manoeuvrability due to their poor turning circle, and also because of growing dissatisfaction with their road-holding ability and proneness to skid in wet weather. On the former subject, the Traffic Commissioner was involved to the extent that, in October 1936, he questioned the desirability of enlarging the Q fleet further on country routes because of their overhang and wide sweep on turning corners. A H Hawkins had apparently become disillusioned with them because their now-reduced seating capacity of 35 offered little advantage over a conventional vehicle, although the official line remained that "no definite decision on policy is to be given at this stage". As early as November 1935 Q 91 was tested against AEC Regal T 232 which showed that the T could turn in 62ft 9ins whereas the Q required 65ft 3ins. With regard to the skidding problem, a later Q – 6Q6-type Q 236 – was despatched for tests at Fort Dunlop on 30th August 1937, the outcome of which was a recommendation that Qs should be fitted with a new design of cross-cut rear tyre to improve road holding. In fact London Transport went further and issued an instruction to garages to fit these all round. That this instruction was sometimes ignored by garage staff was demonstrated when Q 15 was involved in a very bad skidding accident on Holywell Hill, St Albans, in September 1938 and it was found, on subsequent examination, that whilst three tyres had the special cross-cut tread, the fourth was of the old standard pattern.

Such was the lack of stability in their early days that no fewer than 64 of the class were subjected to at least one change of garage during 1936. Leavesden Road garage took the first big hit. With a huge service reorganisation taking place in Watford on 18th March and a smaller one on 4th October, it lost the whole of its 4Q4 quota which had built up to 16 vehicles. Service changes also saw the end of Addlestone's allocation in March as well as Windsor's, although the latter received a few back later in the year, while Dunton Green's all departed with service changes on 3rd September.

The full cost of dismantling the fronts of 100 4Q4s to insert a full-width bulkhead is not known, but it must have been considerable. Converted vehicles could easily be identified from the front because of the provision of new side lights at waist level to replace the small rectangular ones in the front dome, and the insertion of a pair of air intake grilles below the registration plate. Q 6, which appeared in an earlier photograph in as-new condition, is now seen again, still operating from Watford High Street garage but now in rebuilt condition. Photographed in its home town, it deputises for a lowbridge ST on route 336 and temporarily carries a destination blind borrowed from one of the double deckers.
D Evans © Omnibus Society

Northfleet gained its first allocation in March, followed by High Wycombe and Luton in September, although the latter's were despatched elsewhere after only a week. The last garage added to the plus list was Staines, in August. The biggest mass exodus of all, however, occurred as a result of the arrival of 27 brand new Qs of the 5Q5 type between August and November 1936 which saw the removal of all 4Q4s from Amersham, Hatfield, Hertford and St Albans as well as the ones received only a fortnight earlier at High Wycombe.

The 5Q5s had all been intended initially for service with Central Buses, and the reason for diverting some to the Country Bus & Coach department was that London Transport had misjudged its vehicle replacement programme for the Green Line network and now needed to divert 27 4Q4s temporarily to Green Line work. They were needed to displace urgently the same number of obsolete Gilfords still allocated for regular service. In theory, these should have already gone, but because of service revisions and increased duplication requirements it had not been possible to dispense with them. It was acknowledged by management that the 4Q4s were not really suited to Green Line work and that a certain amount of modification would be needed to bring them to the minimum standard acceptable. The total cost of this work would be £1,735 which, as luck would have it, could be covered by an underspending in the originally budgeted purchase cost of Q 6-105. The 27 highest numbered vehicles (Q 81-105, 186, 187) were set aside for conversion into coaches, most of which were delicensed on 1st October 1936 and placed into store pending the conversion work being carried out on them.

While awaiting conversion, however, the seven highest numbered ones were temporarily relicensed for a brief spell of work on Central Buses which seems to have gone almost unnoticed in the annals of London bus history and never to have been photographed. All seven were repainted in red livery, and the first five (Q 101-104) were allocated to Cricklewood garage where they replaced T-types from route 226 on 27th and 28th November 1936. After a further bout of repainting, Q 105 joined them on the 226 and Q 186/187 went

to Kingston on 4th December to work on the 213. This brief episode, which pre-dated the permanent arrival of Qs (of the 5Q5 type) on the 226 by about two years and served at Kingston to temporarily augment its 5Q5 stock, ended at Kingston on 17th February 1937 and Cricklewood on 1st March, after which no further 4Q4s were repainted red until 1948.

The bus-to-coach conversion work on the 4Q4s included alteration to the bodywork to accommodate internal luggage racks, while a forced air heating system similar to one already in use on the later 6Q6 type was installed and was detectable from outside the vehicle by a square-shaped intake grille inserted in the front panel. Brackets were fitted above the windows on both sides to hold standard Green Line style route boards. Upon repainting, the vehicles were given GREEN LINE fleet names, and the B (Bus) suffix following the fleet number was replaced by C (Coach). Unladen weight was shown as increasing from 5tons 12cwt to 6tons 0cwt, and the 27 vehicles were reclassified as 1/4Q4/1. No change appears to have been made to the engine, pump or rear axle settings to accommodate the faster running and general reduction in stopping places that the vehicles would encounter, and from a passenger point of view the retention of the 35 none too comfortable wooden-framed seats would hardly have endeared them for the premium work they were about to undertake.

The start of the 1937 summer programme on 25th March was set as the date on which the 1/4Q4/1s would begin work on Green Line, but a need to replace certain Gilfords earlier than this meant that six (Q 81, 86-88, 95, 98) entered temporary service from Reigate and Hertford just over a fortnight earlier on the 6th. The allocation from 25th March was:

Amersham	MA	5
(Route R Chesham–Oxford Circus)		
Leatherhead	LH	7
(Route O Windsor–Great Bookham)		
Northfleet	NF	8
(Jointly on route A1 Gravesend–Ascot and		
A2 Gravesend–Sunningdale)		

Operation from Leatherhead presumably proved unsatisfactory and from 1st May its Qs were reallocated to High Wycombe (for route Q, High Wycombe–Oxford Circus) and Leavesden Road (route T, Watford–Golders Green). The settled picture during the first half of 1938 saw allocations as follows: Amersham (5), High Wycombe (2), Leavesden Road (4), Northfleet (8), Staines (8). The availability of new 10T10 coaches brought the operation from Northfleet and Staines to an end on 1st August 1938, with the remainder following a month later on 1st September. The vehicles were all reclassified back as buses on their respective changeover dates with the exception of Q 100, which did not stay until the end of the Green Line operation but had been delicensed at Northfleet on 19th July and despatched to Chiswick to serve as an engineering test bed.

General disappointment over the performance of the Qs led, in 1938, to a decision by London Transport's engineers to try improving its design by incorporating a number of modifications in a trial vehicle. Apart from known problems relating to the basic design such as skidding and poor road holding, the Qs were proving to be generally less reliable than had been hoped and were often accused of overheating and of being noisy and prone to vibration. Despite having virtually the same engine and transmission systems as the double deck STL class, and carrying approximately the same unladen weight, they consistently returned inferior fuel consumption figures at an average of 9.30mpg on the STL and 9.08mpg for the Q. Working alongside AEC engineers, a series of improvements was planned and, having dismounted the body, London Transport despatched the chassis of Q 100 to Southall on 12th August 1938 for the planned work to be carried out. It returned to Chiswick on 20th September with a whole range of new fitments, some big and some less so:

1. Flexible instead of solid engine mounting
2. Toroidal direct injection
3. Carden shaft-driven dynamo
4. Repositioned starter and modified leads
5. Modified hand brake linkage
6. Modified starting gear
7. Flexible exhaust pipe
8. Arens cable (throttle control)
9. Repositioned vacuum tank

Apart from the coach classification attached to the fleet number (eg Q 84C) and the appropriate name transfers, each 4Q4 modified for Green Line work could also be immediately identified by the rectangular air intake fitted at the front. As a direct result of this the triangular enamel plate carrying the Board's monogram had to be deleted to make way for the GREEN LINE name transfer. The side route boards were further give-away features, and the decision to mount these parallel with the windows helped to disguise the conspicuous rake of the roof on these vehicles. Q 102, a Staines-based vehicle for the whole of its short Green Line career, was photographed at the main Green Line interchange point at Eccleston Bridge, Victoria, carrying Northfleet (NF) running plates, indicating that it had 'slept out' at the far end of its Ascot-Gravesend run overnight. *G H F Atkins*

In its modified form Q 100 re-entered service at Hertford on 1st January 1939 and was also tried out at Addlestone, High Wycombe and Godstone. At the time it was still officially classified as a coach although now employed on bus services, and in fact it was not until 25th June 1948 that the anomaly was spotted and it once again became Q 100B. By the time the vehicle had been thoroughly tested and accumulated a substantial amount of mileage in its revised form it was June 1941, the nation was in the depths of war, and nothing could be done except to note the results.

Their Green Line days ended, most of the 27 ex-coaches were reallocated to other garages for renewed service bus use, although those at Amersham and High Wycombe stayed where they were and took up bus duties. Most replaced petrol-engine T-type AEC Regals which had come to the end of their service lives. As a result of all these movements, Dunton Green and St Albans renewed their acquaintance with 4Q4s and Crawley and Tring received them for the first time, while a couple joined the fleet at East Grinstead which had been operating the class in growing numbers since January 1937. The constant to-ing and fro-ing normally associated with service changes had seen certain garages lose their 4Q4s in 1937 (Dorking) and 1938 (Dartford, Leatherhead and Swanley), but by the start of 1939 the class was still well dispersed around the Country area as follows:

Addlestone (WY)	11
High Wycombe (HE)	9
Amersham (MA)	11
Northfleet (NF)	6
Crawley (CY)	2
Reigate (RG)	9
Dunton Green (DG)	2
St Albans (SA)	16
East Grinstead (EG)	7
Tring (TG)	1
Godstone (GD)	2
Watford High Street (WA)	11
Guildford (GF)	6
Watford Leavesden Rd (WT)	2
Hertford (HG)	1
Windsor (WR)	6

By the outbreak of war all except five of the 4Q4s were in the latest Country Bus livery of Lincoln green with pale green window frames or were in the process of being painted into it. Q 48, which was new to Leavesden Road but had been at Adddlestone since October 1937, received its new colours in January 1939. *J F Higham © A B Cross*

Even after the regular use of 4Q4s ceased on Green Line work, they still managed to put in occasional appearances whenever more suitable vehicles were unavailable. Although one of the coach conversions might have been more appropriate with their luggage racks, saloon heaters and route boards, Reigate garage is using unconverted Q 11 on this occasion. *A N Porter*

THE 4Q4s in WARTIME AND AFTER

With the outbreak of war expected imminently, blackout and other restrictions were introduced on 1st September 1939. The withdrawal of all Green Line services on that date threw the London Transport fleet into a state of flux with the conversion over a couple of days of a large number of single deckers into temporary ambulances and the commandeering of an even larger quantity of vehicles for evacuation work and troop movements. Being unsuitable for ambulance use because they had no rear door suitable to take stretchers, the 4Q4s were destined to form the backbone of the Country Bus department's operational fleet of large single deck buses throughout the war, but before this nineteen of them from Windsor, Addlestone, Amersham and Leavesden Road garages were hurriedly despatched, along with their drivers, to Victoria Barracks at Windsor on 1st September for temporary use as troop transports.

It was usual for double deckers to be used for this purpose because of their higher carrying capacity and Windsor barracks saw the only sizeable deployment of single deckers. Their work whilst based there took the vehicles on numerous trips to other army establishments within the London area such as the barracks at Regents Park, Chelsea, Woolwich, Coulsdon and the Wellington Barracks in Westminster. They also sometimes went further afield to barracks at places such as Aldershot, Pirbright and Didcot as well as to the rifle ranges at Chobham, Rainham and Purfleet. Unlike many of the Board's double deckers on similar work at this time, none made any really long journeys, the furthest on record being by Q 187 to Birmingham. Most of the nineteen were returned to London Transport in the early hours of 21st September although Q 16, 27 and 87 stayed on until 31st October.

Wartime camouflage measures saw the immediate application of a coat of matt grey point to the roofs of the whole fleet irrespective of what colour they had been previously, as well as the obligatory white blackout markings. Like most of the 4Q4s allocated from new to Watford High Street garage, Q 9 enjoyed an unusually long period of stability and did not leave there until February 1942 when it was transferred to Addlestone. *Omnibus Society*

By a stroke of good fortune none of the 4Q4s were written off or seriously damaged by enemy action and their war service was largely uneventful. Service alterations inevitably occurred from time to time, while a concerted effort was made to convert to double deckers whenever possible to meet increased passenger demand or to effect mileage economies. Major plusses and minuses to record here were the exodus of all 4Q4s from Windsor, Amersham, High Wycombe and Watford High Street garages in 1942 and Hertford in 1943. On the plus side, Godstone resumed operation of the type in 1940 as did Leatherhead in 1942, while Hemel Hempstead joined the ranks of 4Q4 operators for the first time in February 1943, quickly building up a fleet of fifteen such vehicles.

Their constant use throughout the war meant that a regular overhauling programme had to be maintained on the 4Q4s, albeit at wider intervals than in pre-war times. By the time war began most had been overhauled into the latest livery of Lincoln green with pale green window reliefs. Wartime overhauling replaced the pale green with white and subsequently all received the green and white styling. Roofs, which had been repainted from green to grey on the outbreak of war, were changed to brown from 1941 onwards, and it was in this livery styling that the majority of 4Q4s saw out the rest of the war. Nine exceptions were vehicles which, during the course of their scheduled work, operated to factories deemed

strategic to war production. Under a directive issued in August 1942 five 4Q4s based at Addlestone – Q 8, 15, 28, 39, 61 – were repainted in all-over camouflage grey to enable them to serve the strategic Vickers aircraft works in Weybridge, while Q 17, 18, 40, 86 at Reigate were similarly repainted to gain access to the Monotype factory at Salfords which had turned over the whole of its precision engineering capacity to the manufacturing of small arms components. With the easing of restrictions as victory became a real probability, all nine were repainted back into standard green and white between October 1944 and February 1945, but not before Qs 8 and 28 had been transferred to Hemel Hempstead, both still wearing their grey camouflage. The last grey one was Q 17 at Reigate, its reported paint date being 20th February 1945.

A major transformation was carried out on most of the class, however, from December 1941 onwards resulting from an August 1941 announcement by the Minister for War Transport to the Regional Transport Commissioners that they could permit single deckers to be modified as standee vehicles to carry up to a maximum of 30 standing passengers. London Transport was quick to make use of this facility, though only to the extent of carrying 20 standing passengers per bus, which was probably the maximum that it could negotiate with the Transport & General Workers Union.

With typical London Transport thoroughness, even at the height of wartime hostilities, it examined in detail the effect that the carriage of much heavier passenger loads would have on acceleration, braking performance and fuel consumption, and also took into account the additional stresses placed on mechanical capacity and on the general chassis and body structure of various classes of vehicle. As part of this examination, extensive tests were carried out on Q 67, and also on T 12, T 213, T 354 and LT 1195. In the end, the only physical action taken was to increase tyre pressures. One from each type was converted experimentally on 8th December 1941, the 4Q4 selected for this purpose being Q 92 from Addlestone garage. Unlike all the other classes subsequently modified to standee format the 4Q4 could not be fully converted because the raised platforms on which the rear rows of seats were sited prevented the establishment of a flat floor to accommodate standees throughout the vehicle. This meant that thirteen front-facing seats had to

be retained at the rear (two pairs on each side of the gangway and the bench set for five passengers at the back), the official carrying capacity as converted being 32 seated and 20 standing. The unladen weight was revised to 6tons 0cwt, and this continued to be the weight shown on all 4Q4s after the war even after they had been converted back to standard 35 seaters, it probably having been a truer assessment of their real weight all along.

The priority garages to receive standee 4Q4s were Addlestone and Leavesden Road and these were dealt with in January and February 1942. A break in the conversion programme then occurred until July 1942 when the conversion of many more vehicles commenced, lasting into the early part of 1943 with a few further conversions taking place subsequent to this. In total 87 out of the 102 4Q4s became standee vehicles, the fifteen not dealt with being Q 13, 17, 22, 37, 63, 75, 78, 81, 84, 86-88, 91, 98, 100. Ultimately, every garage scheduled to operate 4Q4s had standee vehicles on its books.

Towards the end of 1940 the application of anti-shatter netting to bus windows got under way and a year later paint availability meant that roofs would henceforth be brown instead of grey. Dunton Green-based Q 73 retained pre-war two-tone green livery when photographed and had still to undergo conversion to perimeter seating in August 1942. An unusual embellishment, especially with the war at its height, is a polished ring which someone has taken the trouble to fit to the rear wheel. *C Carter*

Longitudinal seats placed at various levels at the front end of the vehicle, and the retention of normal transverse seating at the rear, were features of the standee 4Q4s. The forward-facing view shows the full-width bulkhead, with centrally-placed door to the driving compartment, fitted in 1936. The presence of overhead luggage racks indicates that this was one of the 1937 conversions for Green Line work, their racks having been left in place when their Green Line stint came to an end.
London Transport Museum

It is interesting to record that, of the various types of single decker modified to standee format, the only ones where physical problems arose because of the heavier passenger loads carried were the Qs on which wheel arches at both front and rear were found to come into contact with the tyres. Exact details are not known but it is possible that, with larger profile tyres fitted than on other classes, clearances within the wheel arches were less generous to start with. During 1945 expenditure of £4,015 was authorised to correct the problem, with the greatest urgency placed on modifying the front wheel arches owing to the possibility of them causing accidents, the rears following on as soon as possible afterwards. The job was eventually overspent by £667 because, when work commenced, it was found necessary to allow for greater clearances than had been originally anticipated. Also, in order to complete the work in the shortest possible time, staff had worked at night on enhanced pay rates and, in some cases, had been paid extra for travelling to distant work locations.

Another modification carried out on the 4Q4s during the war was the fitment of a nearside driver's mirror on each vehicle. In view of their poor nearside visibility from the driving seat, which caused so much disquiet in pre-war years, it is surprising that this fitment took so long to implement and that it required wartime driving conditions to finally bring it about.

When the war in Europe came to a close on 8th May 1945 the 4Q4s were still widely distributed throughout the country fleet and could be found at 14 garages out of the 28 then operational:

Addlestone (WY)	2
Guildford (GF)	7
St Albans (SA)	24
Crawley (CY)	4
H. Hempstead (HH)	12
Tring (TG)	1
Dunton Green (DG)	2
Leatherhead (LH)	10
Watford High St (WA)	1
East Grinstead (EG)	10
Northfleet (NF)	2
W'tf'd Leavesden Rd (WT)	17
Godstone (GD)	3
Reigate (RG)	4

A later wartime scene finds Guildford-based Q 14 loading outside the 18th century Horse & Groom at Merrow for its return journey to Guildford. Now converted to 'standee' layout, Q 14 carries the green and white livery introduced early in the war and subsequently carried through into the post-war era. Q 14 retained its perimeter seating until February 1947.
Alan Nightingale collection

The ubiquitous 4Q4s represented the backbone of London Transport's Country Bus fleet. The list of services which they were scheduled to operate is too widespread and complex to be recorded individually here, but some pockets of intense 4Q4 operation are worth noting, where the class exerted a massive impact on the everyday bus scene. One such case was at St Albans where the local garage held a full quarter of the 4Q4 fleet operating on several major local services and school contracts. An area of particular complexity was in the north-west where Hemel Hempstead and Leavesden Road garages supplied 31 vehicles between them to the jointly-compiled services 307, 307A, 316, 317, 318, 318A, 322 and 337 which included ST, STL and T types but, notably, 12 4Q4s from Hemel Hempstead and 8 from Leavesden Road. At the other end of the scale came the single vehicle at Tring which shared local route 387 with a T, and another at Watford High Street which was not responsible for any scheduled single deck workings but kept a solitary 4Q4 to fulfil a regular contract with the Fairfield Aviation Company.

Three 4Q4s were unlicensed at the war's end. Two were probably awaiting accident repairs but the third, Q 100, was the now highly non-standard vehicle that had been the subject of the pre-war attempt to diagnose and put right all the shortcomings of the Qs in a single vehicle. With the war intervening, this laudable aim had eventually been abandoned and Q 100 was taken out of use in September 1944, since when it had been resident in the Forest Road, Walthamstow store yard. Finally placed back in service in January 1946 during a period of acute vehicle shortage, it was confined to St Albans garage in post-war years and stayed there until its demise at the start of February 1952.

The war's end found the 4Q4s looking well past their prime but still playing a crucial role on Country area services. The overhaul programme continued but with the wartime green and white livery modified by painting the roofs green instead of brown and the mudguards green instead of black. One by one the vehicles with standee seating were converted back to conventional 35-seat layout starting with Q 92 on 23rd November 1945 and ending with Q 89 which last ran in standee form at Leavesden Road on 4th April 1949.

In another typical late-war scene, Q 20 and Q 80 are found in St Albans garage yard, both equipped with full wartime regalia and converted to standee layout. At the time St Albans had the largest allocation of 4Q4s of any garage in the fleet. The red petrol-engined, crash-gearbox STL at the back is a Potters Bar-based vehicle on route 84.
D W K Jones

At a vehicle strength of 102 the 4Q4s represented the largest single batch of Q-types ever built. They played a vital role in keeping services going during the early post-war years and were a familiar sight in many parts of the widely-spread Country Bus territory as shown in these three typical scenes. In the far south-east, Dunton Green's Q 14, which is seen in Sevenoaks bus station along with a vintage AEC Regal of Maidstone & District, was a route 454 'regular' from May 1946 through to November 1949. Associated for even longer with a single garage was Q 30 which ran from Crawley from July 1946 right through to April 1952. It pulls away from East Grinstead town centre just ahead of a Southdown Leyland Tiger working back from a relief run on the company's London express service. In the north, St Albans was a good place to find plenty of Qs in action, and long-time resident Q 92 contrasts in shape to 6Q6 Q 236 as both stop to pick up passengers across the road from the garage. The now-disused roof brackets indicate that both have served as Green Line coaches earlier in their careers, and though Q 92 has long been painted green and white the 6Q6 still carries Green Line colours. *Fred Ivey/Alan B Cross/Alan Nightingale collection*

4Q4s in THE AUSTERITY YEARS

Between March and September 1948 London Transport put into service the first new full-size post-war single deckers specifically intended for bus use with the Country Bus & Coach department since the era of the Q-types. The 30 AEC Regals comprising the 15T13 class (T 769-798) inevitably had an immediate impact on the 4Q4s, notably at Hemel Hempstead and Leavesden Road garages into which all the new Ts were assimilated. The result was a complete clear-out of Qs from Hemel Hempstead, with the last one leaving in August 1948, along with a partial reduction at Leavesden Road. This did not put a final end to 4Q4s at Hemel Hempstead as, in typical Country Bus fashion, odd ones returned in 1949 and 1950. In fact stray 4Q4s appeared at, and sometimes disappeared quickly from, various garages in the late 1940s and early 1950s including Epping, Grays, Luton, Swanley and Watford High Street, usually in response to schedule changes or new services.

The main fall-out from the arrival of the 30 new Ts was twofold. Chelsham garage, not previously a 4Q4 user, took in an allocation of ten on 20th May 1948 and remained a user of them until the main demise of the class four years later. The second manoeuvre was much more radical. It had been decided that, in order to provide much-needed additional single deck rolling stock on Central Buses, sufficient 4Q4s would be repainted red to convert the whole of route 233 at West Green to this type of vehicle, allowing its 5Q5s to be redeployed to ease vehicle availability problems elsewhere. The reason for converting the whole route was to avoid the undesirability of having front and centre entrance Qs running together, and it meant that eleven red 4Q4s were required of which five were selected to start with. Q 44 which was already in the works for routine overhaul was finished in red, while Q 8, 53, 67, 68 were taken straight out of service at Hemel Hempstead and Leavesden Road during the first week of August and given a quick repaint into Central Bus colours. The visual effect on all five was considerable. Unlike the Country Bus & Coach department, Central Buses had been attempting to modernise its Qs (the 5Q5s)

by repainting them into a revised livery of all-over red relieved by cream mouldings above and below the windows, eliminating the white window frames and brown roof, and this transformed their appearance. This same approach was now taken with the five 4Q4s which looked very smart and unusual when freshly repainted.

The five entered service at West Green between 11th and 18th August 1948. Almost immediately discontent with them broke out amongst the normally placid staff at this garage, and this was perhaps unsurprising. Route 233's journey between Wood Green trolleybus depot and Finsbury Park and back involved negotiating an unusually high number of right angle turns or sharper, and whilst the drivers were happy to work with the 5Q5s because they could clearly see the nearside corners through the open doorway, the notoriously poor nearside visibility on the 4Q4s was now declared to be hazardous, especially during hours of darkness.

With these complaints ringing in its mind, the management quickly re-thought its plans and arranged for the next two vehicles to be painted red to go instead to Dalston garage for route

The 4Q4s at West Green garage newly repainted red for the start of their introduction to Central Bus service included Q 8, with two more following soon afterwards and all carrying a livery style completely new to this type of vehicle. Photographed in the gloomy surroundings of the Finsbury Park terminus, the shine seems to have worn off very rapidly from Q 8 even though it has only been in service since repainting for less than three months.
Alan B Cross

208A. These arrived at Dalston on 21st September (Q 65) and 18th October 1948 (Q 85), and the five from West Green joined them there on 15th November. However, Dalston was probably not the wisest choice to have made. Its union branch was renowned for being probably the most militant in the fleet, and when the Dalston drivers also took a dislike to the 4Q4s their fate on Central Buses was sealed, for the time being at least. During February and March 1949 they were all returned to Country Buses where six of the seven resumed immediate service, still in red livery, while the remaining one (Q 67) was sent for overhaul back into green before being used again.

Four out of the remaining six red Qs (Q 8, 53,

63, 85) were despatched to Tring garage, its first allocation of 4Q4s in post-war years, from which Q 53 passed to Watford High Street, still in red livery, in October of the same year to renew that garage's acquaintance with 4Q4s and to enable it to introduce new route 332. The other two red 4Q4s duly turned up at Reigate, passing six months later to Chelsham and then, after a few days, to Northfleet.

Service changes to meet evolving traffic patterns within the Country area, including further substitution of double deckers for single deckers where possible, resulted in a decreased demand for 4Q4s by the end of the decade. At the start of the summer programme on 18th May 1949

Banishment from the Central area in 1949 found Q 65 reallocated to Reigate where it ran alongside but looked very different from the regular green 4Q4s on the busy 447. Q 65 later served in red livery at Chelsham and Northfleet before returning to the Central area at Kingston in February 1950. *Surfleet negative collection* © *D Clark*

only 67 out of the 102 were scheduled for Monday to Friday service which, allowing for overhaul and maintenance spares of around 15%, would only come to a total requirement for about 77 buses.

As it happened, some garages, notably Leavesden Road, held well above their normal level, perhaps as an insurance against growing unreliability through advancing age. Garages and services scheduled for 4Q4 operation on 18th May are listed below, but in addition to the garages on this list, single unscheduled 4Q4s were held at Godstone, Hemel Hempstead and Windsor garages, presumably to act as spares for other types of vehicle or to serve as Green Line reliefs.

Although it had been a big user of 4Q4s in pre-war years, single deckers of any sort seldom appeared at Watford High Street garage after the war. A short-lived exception was when new route 332 was introduced on 5th October 1949 necessitating the allocation of a lone 4Q4 which was this garage's only single decker. Q 14 departed from there in November 1950 following the double decking of the 332 with STLs. *D A Thompson*

Chelsham (CM)	3	403/A	Wallington-Tonbridge etc (plus 1 STL and1 C)
	3	453	Warlingham-Caterham
Crawley (CY)	1	426	Crawley circular
	5	434	Horsham-Dormansland (plus 1 STL)
Dunton Green (DG)	1	454	Chipstead-Tonbridge (plus 1 STL)
East Grinstead (EG)	8	424	Reigate-East Grinstead
Northfleet (NF)	3	489/A	Gravesend-Ash/Meopham
Reigate (RG)	1	406C	Earlswood-Kingswood
	1	414	West Croydon-Horsham (plus 8 STL)
	2	440/A	Redhill-Salfords/Redstone Estate
	10	447/A/B	Reigate-Woldingham etc.
St Albans (SA)	12	365/391/A	St Albans-Luton/Harpenden
	1	382	St Albans-Codicote
	5		Supplementary schedules
Tring (TG)	2	301/C	Watford-Aylesbury etc (plus 6 RT)
	2	387	Tring-Aldbury
Watford (WT)	3	309	Rickmansworth-Uxbridge (plus 3T)
(Leavesden Road)	3	318/A	Watford-Chipperfield/Two Waters (plus 8T)

Starting on 6th February 1950 a further attempt was made to gain acceptance for 4Q4s on Central Bus operation, but this time the garage selected was Kingston whose range of semi-rural services stretching well into country districts offered a much greater chance of acceptance by operating staff. A programme of heavy renovation (which amounted almost to complete rebodying) of really elderly LT class single deckers was under way, but some were beyond redemption and redundant Qs were needed to fill the gap left by their departure. After hosting a couple of vehicles for training and testing for a few weeks, regular operation of 4Q4s from Kingston commenced later in February, their usual spheres of operation being routes 215 and 219 which took them to Ripley and Weybridge respectively. Kingston's Q fleet had finally stabilised by 1st May 1950 at 14 vehicles, including those former West Green/Dalston vehicles which were still in red livery plus Q 6 and Q 26 which were repainted red in April and June 1950, making a total of eight red Qs on Kingston's books. The remainder stayed green.

With the delivery of new RF single deckers on the horizon the overhaul programme for the 4Q4s gradually drew to a close, leaving

On 13th January 1950 a small allocation of 4Q4s was officially renewed at Leatherhead when two out of the three workings on route 419 were converted from T types. Only LH54 on the time schedule officially stayed with Ts because of inter-working with other services, although this arrangement was obviously not strictly complied with as, on this occasion at least, it is being covered by Q 47. Presumably Leatherhead was suffering a vehicle shortage at the time as Q 47 was not one of its own allocation but was on loan from Reigate.

Looking resplendent, having just emerged from its seventh and final overhaul on 26th April 1950, Q 6 has now adopted red livery for the first time and has acquired a route stencil holder above the window immediately behind the entrance door. It stands outside its new base at Kingston in the company of STL 1339, now demoted to learner duties after its body was condemned in June 1949. *Alan B Cross*

some unoverhauled after 1947/48. The final few overhauls, conducted between November 1950 and January 1951, resulted in four vehicles emerging in the 'all green' colours now standard for the whole fleet, which as far as the 4Q4s were concerned was a green version of the red scheme used on 4Q4s since 1948 except that the mudguards were not picked out in black. At least two others were repainted into this style in 1951 without undergoing full overhaul and more might have been similarly dealt with that have gone unnoticed.

The first 288 RFs scheduled to enter service between April 1951 and the autumn of 1952 were all destined for the private hire and Green Line fleets, leaving vehicles specifically designed for country bus work not due until the spring of 1953. However, it was not London Transport's intention to keep the 4Q4s in service as long as this. The class was now regarded as obsolete, indeed with just a very few exceptions London Transport was the only operator anywhere in the country still running Qs. The decision was taken to replace the 4Q4s with 10T10 and TF vehicles downgraded from Green Line work as soon as these became available.

The withdrawal programme began on 18th February 1952 when Qs were removed from Tring and Hemel Hempstead. Thereafter, withdrawals swept through the Country area thick and fast

Although they were now nearing the end of their days a very few 4Q4s emerged from overhaul from August 1950 onwards painted in the latest Country Bus livery, which resembled the styling used on red vehicles since 1948 except that the mudguards were not picked out separately in black. Q 29 was a November 1950 overhaul which spent its last two operational months at East Grinstead on the 424. It had just three more days' service ahead of it when photographed on 27th April 1952. *Allen T Smith © A B Cross*

with the result that, after 1st September of the same year, the only Country Bus garage with an allocation of 4Q4s was Reigate which still had seventeen on its books. The replacement of these would have to wait until 1953 when the first of the department's new RF buses would become available.

On Central Buses, the withdrawal of 4Q4s at Kingston became a protracted affair dependent upon the availability of TDs to replace Qs after themselves having been replaced by new RFs. From 14 in service at the start of September the figure had dwindled to 11 (5 green and 6 red) by 1st January 1953. Withdrawals continued with the last red one, Q 44, reaching the end of the road on 12th February. The final two green Qs in service at Kingston, Qs 42 and 64, were both withdrawn on 25th March 1953.

The very last 4Q4s continued running at Reigate for about a fortnight longer before these, too, were withdrawn. A substantial exodus occurred on 7th April 1953 when ten were delicensed (including Q 55 which had been selected as the future museum bus), leaving the final six theoretically available

Northfleet garage was positioned fairly early in the 1952 Q-type replacement programme, and the six 4Q4s that remained there to the end were all withdrawn from service on 1st March 1952. One of the final survivors there, Q 35, is seen near the end of its days with Queen Victoria apparently perched on its roof as it pulls to a halt outside the old Gravesend Technical College.
D A Jones

St Albans, which had been a major centre for Q-type operation for many years, ceased to echo to them on 25th March 1952 when its last nine 4Q4s were delicensed. Q 98 carried a livery tried out briefly on Country area vehicles of various classes in 1948 in which the white relief was replaced by cream with the latter applied solely to the areas immediately surrounding the windows of the passenger saloon. As a former coach, Q 98 was a rarity in having been embellished at some time in its later days with an enamel triangle badge above its front grille leaving only just enough space below it for the LONDON TRANSPORT transfer.

Despite the influx of new RFs, Kingston remained an outpost of 4Q4 operation right up to the start of 1953 and Q 15 managed to hang on almost until the very end, being withdrawn from service on 1st March. Although it had been at Kingston since March 1950 it had, like various others, remained in green and white livery and had, in fact, not undergone a proper overhaul since July 1947. Special Kingston adornments are the route number stencil holder next to the doorway and the 'minimum fares' board below it. RT 25, standing nearby, is typical of the RT2s which dominated route 85 at the time. *Alan B Cross*

On a busy Saturday in July 1952 red Q 8, which is already almost fully laden, picks up even more passengers heading into Kingston at the compulsory stop in Esher. Q 8 was one of the red 4Q4s that inaugurated their unsuccessful introduction on route 233 back in August 1948 and had remained red ever since. It was a very rare case (possibly the only one) of a 4Q4 with a divided back window, probably a relic from the wartime years. *Ken Blacker*

As their final days drew near and Kingston's Qs approached seventeen years of age their frailties and general obsolescence began to become apparent, especially when compared with the silent smoothness and general opulence of the Q1 trolleybuses such as the one Q 20 is pursuing through Kingston on this occasion. Carrying red livery since April 1950, Q 20 was one of the earliest of Kingston's Qs to cease operation when it was sent for storage in Lea Bridge trolleybus depot in August 1952. *C Carter*

for operation for two more days before being delicensed on the 9th. These were Q 23, 70, 71, 86, 97, 105 but it is not known which, if any, of them actually ran on the theoretical last day.

However, the story had not quite finished. 1953 was the year of Queen Elizabeth II's coronation, and to cater for the anticipated demand fluctuations during the key month of June many time expired and now redundant buses were temporarily relicensed from 1st June up to the end of the month and allocated to a variety of garages in case they were needed. This included ten of the 4Q4s which had been active at Reigate in April, and these were distributed amongst six garages:- East Grinstead (Q 9), Guildford (Q19), Leatherhead (Q 22), Reigate (Q 60), Staines (Q 70-72, 86, 97) and Windsor (Q 105). It is not known which, if any, of them were actually called into use during the month.

Inroads into the 4Q4 ranks had first been made in April 1952 when London Transport arranged for twelve to be dismantled by Cohen's who returned their chassis to Chiswick for dismantling as a source of spare parts for vehicles still in the fleet. Sales of complete buses, mostly to dealers, began at the end of 1952. As far as is known only two saw further stage carriage service in the UK, both in County Durham, with Q 23 running on the G&B co-operative in the ownership of Gillett Brothers of Quarrington Hill and Q 105 on Blenkinsop's Scarlet Band service at West Cornforth. Many were used as staff transports by contractors and a few became shops or caravans. A few were exported, the most notable destination being Libya where no

fewer than six (Q 10, 20, 21, 34, 53, 78) were in the UTA (Uniona Tripolina Autotransporti) fleet in Tripoli while Q 96 was with another Tripoli operator. Q 103 became a familiar sight in Malta for some years and Q 31 (at least) was in Cyprus.

London Transport itself retained two vehicles. As recorded above, Q 55 was placed in the museum fleet and today is owned by the London Transport Museum. Q 75 was converted in August 1952 into an 8-seater mobile gas unit for London Transport's Civil Defence organisation, its role being to demonstrate various means of decontamination and protection following a nerve gas attack. In November 1955 it was transferred into the miscellaneous vehicle fleet and numbered 1035CD (although displaying the fictitious fleet number Q 1035!) and was finally disposed of in July 1964.

Two London Transport Qs survive for posterity as museum pieces although it is perhaps slightly unfortunate that both are 4Q4s and nothing survives of the 5Q5 or 6Q6 series. In addition to Q 55, mentioned above, Q 83 is very much alive on the preservation scene. Initially sold by London Transport to the Sutton Coldfield Old People's Welfare Committee, it subsequently passed into private preservation and is now owned by the London Bus Museum at Brooklands. A third 4Q4, Q 69, was also taken into preservation after it was no longer required by the Gravesend Old People's Welfare Committee, but unfortunately its private owner allowed it to deteriorate to a point of no return after which the chassis was used to supply spare parts for Q 83.

Route 447 was the last bastion of 4Q4 operation, and in this typical latter day scene Q 22 and Q 38 are seen passing in Redhill. Q 22 was one of a number made available, after normal withdrawal, for operation in Coronation Week 1953, in this case at Leatherhead garage, but it is not known if its services were called upon.
Alan B Cross

The British Railways large enamel sign leaves no doubt as to the city where this photograph of Q 40 was taken. Withdrawn from service at Crawley on 16th April 1952, it had passed via a dealer to railway infrastructure contractor Grant Lyon & Co Ltd. The photograph was taken in Great Bridgewater Street in May 1957, nearly four years after leaving London, by which time the sight of an AEC Q on any form of active service within the UK had become a real rarity. *J S Cockshott*

Tripoli, the Libyan capital, was a good place to find ex-London Transport Q types, where at least eleven (seven of which were 4Q4s) were imported in 1953/54 by three different operators. The largest operator in Tripoli, with the biggest fleet of Qs, was UTA (Unione Tripolina Autotrasporti) where Qs 21 and 10 are seen contrasting greatly in appearance with a contemporary Lancia. Both Qs retained right hand drive but their old entrance was neatly removed and replaced by the former emergency door on the opposite side. *Brian Parnell*

Probably the best remembered of the 4Q4s exported to work overseas was the former Q 103 which ran on a fairly steady basis in Malta from 1953 right through to about January 1968, and was long associated with the busy route from the capital, Valetta, to Birkirkara. With its bulky appearance and rounded contours it looked so much more modern than the locally-bodied rolling stock which then prevailed, such as the Reo ahead it on the stand at the Birkirkara terminus, and from at least 1964 it was adorned with a Bedford SB radiator grille and a chromium-plated front bumper. *Bob Burrell*

Preserved for posterity are Q 55 and Q 83, seen standing side by side outside the London Bus Museum at Brooklands and representing, respectively, the 4Q4 marque which spent their entire working lives as buses and the 1/4Q4/1 Green Line coach variant. The latter vehicle retains its front air intake but now carries an AEC style triangular badge, which it did not do after its coach conversion, whereas Q 55 has lost its badge as, indeed, it had in its later operating days. Q 83 has appeared in various versions of green livery but was in Central Bus red from 2002 until 2017 although it was never actually painted red in 'real life'. *David Thrower*

THE 5Q5 BATCH: Q 106 – Q 185

Almost immediately after placing the official order for the 4Q4s, attention turned to the provision of a new fleet of single deckers for the Central Bus department. First priority was the replacement of 31 obsolete vehicles (13 S type, 1 LS, 10 DE and 7 LN), to which the department wished to add a further 49 vehicles, a truly huge number that it considered would become necessary to cater for the introduction of new services and for enhancements on existing ones, bringing the grand total to 80. Once again the Board's engineers placed great faith in the Q chassis, albeit in a modified form to better suit Central Bus requirements. The 80 vehicles that were subsequently ordered and were classified as 5Q5 in the Chiswick system, differed fundamentally from the standard Q-type chassis as adopted for single deckers in having a much longer front overhang, and a consequentially shorter wheelbase, in order to accommodate the entrance door ahead of the front wheels. In this respect the 5Q5s closely resembled the standard double deck Q chassis in their basic layout, albeit with a 16ft 5ins wheelbase as against the 15ft 10ins of the double decker, producing an overall

length of 27ft 6ins compared with the double decker's 26ft 0ins. The 80 5Q5s were, in fact, the only single deck Qs ever produced by AEC with entrance positioned ahead of the front wheels.

By 15th February 1935 development plans for the new bus were sufficiently advanced for A A M Durrant to present them to a meeting of the Engineering Committee. These showed a 37-seater with minimum seat spacing of 2ft 4¼ins, and were accepted apart from a few minor alterations such as a modified step arrangement at the loading platform and the provision of armrests on the longitudinal seats. In March formal tenders were issued and all-metal bodywork was specified as it had been previously with the 4Q4s. Park

Q 117 was one of the vehicles allocated from new to Dalston garage for route 208, one of the most heavily used of London Transport's single deck services particularly at rush hours. Like all the Dalston 5Q5 fleet it was swept away on 1st June 1938 to provide up-to-date rolling stock for the prestigious new 233 operation over the new road through the grounds of Alexandra Palace for which London Transport had contributed towards the cost. The small advertisement label on the rear panel extols "The Country by Green Line". *Alan Nightingale collection*

Royal was the successful tenderer to supply the bodies at a total cost of £60,000, AEC's quote for the provision of the 80 Q chassis having been £78,000. A delivery schedule drawn up with the two manufacturers specified a sample chassis to be delivered to Park Royal's works on 5th November 1935 for completion of the bodywork by 9th December, with full scale construction commencing at a rate of three vehicles per week starting one month later and concluding with the final deliveries on 20th April 1936.

As well as differing from the 4Q4s through the already-mentioned variations in chassis frame, floor height, wheelbase length and associated mechanical modifications, the 5Q5 also had a revised engine. This was the improved Comet Mk III version of the A170 which had a slightly reduced cylinder bore of 105mm, resulting in an output of 7.585 litres, with maximum power output reduced from the former 115bhp at 2,500rpm to 95bhp at 1,800rpm. Still genetically referred to as the AEC 7.7, this slightly lower performance unit was claimed to achieve better fuel consumption as well as being quieter, although the latter feature was not always readily apparent!

The allocated fleet numbers Q 106-185 followed directly on from the 4Q4s, and included amongst their number was one bus that differed from the rest. This was Q 151 which was built with a 1 inch longer wheelbase (at 16ft 6ins) whilst its overall body length was reduced by 1 inch to 27ft 5ins. The difference was all confined to the rear end of the vehicle and resulted in the already short rear overhang looking shorter than ever. The reasons for specifying these changes have been lost in the mists of time, but in all probability they were part of a trial in redistributing weight around the rear axle to see if this would achieve improved road holding and reduce the risk of skidding to which the Q-type was known to be prone. Q 151 received the unique classification 1/5Q5/1 and, though non-standard compared with the rest of the batch, it managed to achieve a working life fully comparable with all the others.

One of the first pair of 5Q5s to arrive at Chiswick from Park Royal was Q 109 (along with Q 108) on 19th December 1935. It spent some months thereafter undergoing a lengthy series of tests which meant that it was not licensed until 21st May 1936, entering passenger service at Merton five days later. It is seen on trade plates undergoing testing with a distance measuring wheel attached. Interestingly, the fleet numbers on these early arrivals were displayed on the front panels, as on double decks Q2 and Q 3, but this practice soon ceased and it is probable that no 5Q5s entered service like this.

Merton's Q 110, photographed at Raynes Park, was one of the very first of its type to be placed into service, on 4th March 1936, providing slightly greater seating capacity than the six-wheeled LT single deckers formerly used on route 200. An unusual feature on these vehicles was that the offside route number stencil was placed behind glass, accessed from within the driver's cab. *J F Higham © A B Cross*

The standard fleet number position is demonstrated on Q 129, a January 1936 delivery, and this is where it remained throughout the active lives of these vehicles. Q 129 was fitted out for this official photograph fully blinded and plated for route 223 from Uxbridge garage which was an odd choice as Uxbridge was never allocated any 5Q5s and the 223 was, at that time, a one-man service operated by Dennis Darts. *London Transport Museum*

Although the concept of a raked roof line was perpetuated on the 5Q5s it was accommodated more harmoniously than on the 4Q4s and the whole design was much more stylish. Q 120 was an addition to Merton's original 5Q5 allocation to permit conversion of route 225 from one-man DA operation on 29th April 1936. It stands at the weekday terminus in Lower Morden of its far from hectic 6 minute run to Raynes Park. *London Transport Museum*

The RF class, which replaced the 5Q5s almost two decades later, barely represented any improvement over them in terms of styling, accessibility and comfort, so ultra-modern for its time was the design of the 5Q5. The interiors of the two bore many similarities, and because of its raised floor line there was no need for the rear end seats to be placed on plinths in the 5Q5 as they had been on the 4Q4s. Nor was the same sense of diminishing headroom so apparent when walking towards the rear.
London Transport Museum

Apart from a general family likeness when viewed directly from the front, the body designed by the Chiswick team for the 5Q5 bore virtually no resemblance to the 4Q4. In order to give better coverage over the wheel arches and to achieve a completely flat profile, the saloon floor was raised, and this resulted in an increase in the overall body height of 6¼ inches to 9ft 11ins. The increased height gave the vehicles a more squat and sturdy appearance when viewed externally, while a reduction in the number of saloon side windows from seven to five made the body appear shorter whereas, in reality, both types were of the same overall length. The design retained AEC's concept of a raked roof, still dipping down from front to rear but now with a more subdued slope, and the sloping effect was further reduced by placing the drip moulding at a constant height above the windows instead of following the roof contour as had been done on the 4Q4s. The positioning of the saloon entrance ahead of the front axle immediately to the left of the driver predated the general adoption of this layout for single deckers by a full decade and a half, and the absence of a door to seal the entrance while the vehicle was in motion, whilst being a feature common with double deck Q bodies built to this layout, happened to coincide with then-current Metropolitan Police rules prohibiting the fitment of such doors on stage carriage vehicles. Unlike the 4Q4s the emergency exit was placed in the rear wall of the vehicle, and it was the absence of doorways from midway along both sides that helped to make the window spacing so much neater and less fussy-looking than on the 4Q4.

Internally the Park Royal bodies followed the now-established London Transport practice with regard to items such as window cappings and general décor, but the latest style of aluminium alloy seat frames was employed resulting in a much improved overall appearance. The seating layout allowed ample space at the front of the passenger saloon for standing passengers and general circulation, with an inward-facing bench seat for three on the nearside immediately behind the doorway, plus two adjoining seats, both for three passengers, on the offside above the engine

cover. Beyond these, conventional transverse seating resulted in eight pairs of seats on the nearside and six on the offside, giving a grand total of 37. A novel innovation was the introduction of half drop windows which could be wound up and down instead of relying on pinch clips, the winding handles being mounted in a central position above each window. This was a design developed by London Transport itself and referred to internally as the 'top channel control type', and it was subsequently used on various other single deck classes purchased by the Board during pre-war years. The windows for most of the 5Q5s were made by Rawlings Machine Company of Balham although six 5Q5s (numbers unknown) had half drop windows by Birmingham manufacturer Hallam, Sleigh & Cheston of their own design at a cost saving of £29.14s.0d per body.

In accordance with their intended use on Central Bus services, the bodywork contract for the 5Q5s specified that they should all be painted in standard red and white livery, but retaining the black roof originally introduced on Q 1 with a sweep-down at the rear to waistrail level. However this plan was changed while the batch was under construction, with a revised requirement that the final 27 from the production line should be delivered in Country area green. As explained earlier, 27 4Q4s had to be diverted as a matter of urgency on to Green Line work and, fortuitously, the same number of new 5Q5s could be diverted straight off the production line to act as their temporary replacements. In hindsight, it appears that the Central Bus department had, in any case, heavily over-estimated the number of additional single deckers likely to be needed for service expansion, so the non-availability of these 27 vehicles was unlikely to cause any immediate problem. The vehicles delivered in green were Q 151, 152, 155, 159, 162-164, 166-185.

Not unexpectedly, deliveries of the new vehicles did not go exactly in line with the originally agreed time scale, with deliveries running about three months late on average. When they arrived, the 80 5Q5s were licensed as CLE 129-208, with chassis numbers 0762182-0762261 and London Transport body numbers 16151-16230, all in strict numerical sequence. The first to be allocated to garages were Q 110 and 115 at Merton and Q 108 and 112 at Dalston, all on 4th March 1936, and it can be assumed that they entered service on or soon after these dates. Chalk Farm followed from 25th March, with Old Kent Road from 1st May and Kingston and Harrow Weald later in the same month. Between them, these six garages absorbed all 53 red 5Q5s. Most were employed, either directly or through inter-garage transfers, in replacing obsolete vehicles, although those at Merton were for an extension of route 200 and to replace a DA class Dennis Dart on route 225, while those at Kingston permitted the introduction of new route 255.

After the last red vehicle, Q 156, entered service at Kingston on 8th June there was a lapse of almost two months before the green ones were required, during which time new arrivals were stored unlicensed at a variety of locations including Chiswick tram depot and country garages at Reigate, Hertford and Hemel Hempstead. The first day that any of them came into use was 1st

August 1936 when six were licensed at Northfleet, seven at Hatfield and four at Hertford. These were subsequently augmented to eight each at Hatfield and Hertford, along with five at Amersham which received its first 5Q5s on 1st September. Some of these allocations did not prove to be permanent, the first transfers out being Amersham's which all went to High Wycombe on 1st October, quickly followed by Northfleet's which departed for St Albans just over a week later on the 9th. Presumably the vehicles had been found unsuitable at their original locations, leading to the necessity for more permanent homes to be found for them.

After only a comparatively short time in service, a structural defect became apparent with the floor bearers on the Park Royal bodywork, and in November 1936 Q 130 was returned to the builders for examination. Modifications were made to Q 130 which presumably were found to have cured the problem under service conditions, and as a result the remainder were all sent back to Park Royal, a vehicle at a time, for rectification between May and October 1937.

Green liveried 5Q5s first entered service on 1st August 1936 and Q 171 was one of this original contingent. Route 341 was their first venture in the northern part of the Country Bus area and both Hatfield and Hertford garages received an allocation for their joint operation on this and route 330. Although carrying Hatfield garage plates, having overnighted there, Q 171 is in fact a Hertford vehicle. It is notable that, although less than three months old, much of the shine has already worn off its main green panels. This particular paint was notable for its poor wearing qualities and was replaced two years later by the darker and more durable Lincoln green. *J F Higham © A B Cross*

A fair amount of management time was spent at Board level during 1936 over the question of whether or not dummy radiators should be displayed on the front of Q-type vehicles. This appears to have arisen from a complaint received by Frank Pick that, with Qs having a similar appearance front and back, it was difficult to know in which direction they were travelling! This seemingly spurious complaint was taken so seriously that discussions took place about providing a dummy radiator, perhaps in the form of a painted outline, on the front of each Q-type vehicle. In pursuance of this, green Q 168, which had yet to enter passenger service, was inspected during July 1936 with a dummy radiator attached, and it was initially proposed that 51 Qs still to be constructed (Q 188-238) should be fitted with these. Sketches were drawn up of various designs of dummy radiator, only for common sense to prevail at a Chairman's meeting on 24th September when it was minuted that "up to the present no particular difficulty had arisen over the general similarity of the front and rear of the Q type vehicles and it was therefore decided that no steps would be taken to fit dummy radiators for the time being". Presumably the dummy radiator was then removed from Q 168 before it entered service, but the matter had not completely died and the subsequent story relating to 'radiators' on Q 2 and others is told in an earlier chapter.

A problem that was real rather than imagined manifested itself very early in the working lives of the 5Q5s, namely the high number of passenger accidents, many of which related to the positioning of the open doorway ahead of the front wheels. This led to comparative tests being carried out at Chiswick early in 1937 between a 5Q5 and various other types of bus. These tests revealed that, on the 5Q5, a sudden movement of the steering wheel by the driver could cause a loss of balance at speeds as low as 3 mph whereas, on the STL with its rear entrance, such conditions had no appreciable effect. When negotiating a normal right-angled offside turn, loss of balance occurred at speeds of 5 mph or greater on the 5Q5 as compared with 7 mph on the STL, the over-balancing force becoming proportionately greater as the speed increased. London Transport was sufficiently worried to warn its staff periodically, via the internal 'Traffic Circular', that if it became necessary for a 5Q5 to be 'piloted' by the conductor – which would normally be when reversing – he must not attempt to leave or board the vehicle while in motion. Matters came to a head in March 1938 when a passenger by the name of Ernest Gundry died after falling from the platform of one of Old Kent Road's 5Q5s on route 202. The incident straight away resulted in an investigation into whether a movable barrier could be inserted at the entrance of the 5Q5s, but this was found impracticable. However an experiment was approved in July 1938, specifically for route 202, whereby buses should not be moved until the conductor had collected all the fares so that he could be in position on the platform whenever the vehicle was in motion. The experiment required an assessment of what additional running times and consequential increase in operating costs would be involved, and it is not known if this trial was, in fact, ever conducted or its eventual outcome.

The years 1937 and 1938 saw further manoeuvring between garages of the Country area 5Q5s. On 8th July 1937 the complete High Wycombe contingent moved to Watford High Street, but this did not work out particularly well. The Watford drivers were quick to complain on health grounds, the problem being that the duty schedule required crews to work part of their shift on R class AEC Reliances, on which the cabs were very hot due to their closeness to the engine exhaust manifold, and the other part of the shift on 5Q5s where the cab was very cold and draughty. The problem was only alleviated by moving the 5Q5s once again, this time to Windsor, on 1st August 1938. St Albans' last 5Q5s were also moved out on this date, some to Windsor and others to Hertford. Meanwhile Dorking and Guildford had both received 5Q5s on 3rd November 1937 as the Metropolitan Traffic Commissioner was not prepared to allow the operation of 4Q4s (or the later 6Q6 coaches) on route 425 between the two towns, although he would accept 5Q5s because of their much improved nearside vision of kerbs and corners from the driver's seat.

On 1st August and 1st September 1938 the 27 4Q4s temporarily transferred to Green Line work were released from these duties, theoretically freeing the release of the green 5Q5s to take up their originally intended role on Central Buses. In fact only four vehicles were required there at this time. Q 181, 183-185 were repainted red between 6th and 10th October 1938, leaving the remaining 23 active within the Country Bus & Coach department until further red repaints were required in 1942. The four vehicles for repainting came from the Windsor allocation, which was subsequently entirely eliminated on 30th January 1939 when its final three 5Q5s were reallocated to Guildford.

The immediate need for additional Qs on Central Buses was brought about by the introduction on 12th October 1938 of an extension to Chalk Farm-worked route 231 (Hampstead Heath-Harlesden) southwards to Kew Green. This extra work was allocated to Willesden garage which received Qs for the first time, three from Kingston plus the four vehicles newly repainted red. This resulted in the end of Qs at Kingston, albeit only temporarily until a couple were received on 1st February 1939, with many more later in the same year. Even before this, a major vehicle exchange had occurred in north London on 1st June 1938 to allow West Green garage to receive an intake of 13 5Q5s to coincide with an extension of route 233 (Finsbury Park-Alexandra Park) through the private grounds of Alexandra Palace over a new roadway towards which London Transport had contributed part of the cost, to a new terminus at Wood Green. The extended 233, now worked by the newest type of single decker in the fleet, was effectively a belated replacement of two single deck tram services that had previously served the Alexandra Palace grounds until their withdrawal on 23rd February 1938, and whereas the two tram routes had not met up, the 233 provided a through facility for the first time. The Qs employed on it were obtained from Dalston garage, which received LTs in their place and did not regain a Q allocation until almost the end of 1941.

One final event involving the 5Q5s prior to the outbreak of war was the reallocation of Willesden's operation on route 231 to Cricklewood on 7th June 1939. On the day that war officially broke out, 3rd September 1939, the allocation of the 80 5Q5s to garages was as follows:

Central Buses			Country Buses		
Chalk Farm (CF)	11		Dorking (DS)	3	
Cricklewood (W)	7		Guildford (GF)	5	
Harrow Weald (HD)	9		Hatfield (HF)	8	
Kingston (K)	2		Hertford (HG)	7	
Merton (AL)	5				
Old Kent Road (P)	10				
West Green (WG)	13				

Some early Country Bus operations involving 5Q5s quickly proved unsuccessful leading, in October and November 1936, to eleven of them from Northfleet and Hertford being redeployed at St Albans. This particular vehicle, Q 179, was received from Hertford on 5th November 1936. It was photographed in the bus station built as an integral part of the splendid new garage in St Albans which had only been brought into use as recently as 26th August of that year.
D W K Jones

THE 5Q5s IN WARTIME AND AFTER

Wartime conditions were destined to bring some quite big changes to the 5Q5s and their spheres of operation although, in common with the 4Q4s, the whole batch was destined to survive the war relatively unscathed. As early as 1st November 1939 route 231 was converted to double deckers (and renumbered 70), whereupon the whole of Chalk Farm's allocation of 5Q5s moved south to Kingston. At Cricklewood, however, Qs remained to run a special railway replacement service between Edgware and Finchley (and also to work route 226 from November 1940). On 6th March 1940 Sidcup garage commenced running Qs to ease overcrowding conditions on route 241, with most of its intake of eleven coming from Kingston, whose Q allocation diminished to almost nothing and finally disappeared completely in August 1941. Q operation resumed in a small way at Dalston on 17th February 1941 and increased notably between 9th and 14th March 1942 when eight Qs, formerly at St Albans, were repainted from green to red (Q 151, 159, 162, 167, 170, 172, 173, 175). Shortly before this, during January 1942, two other green Qs (Q 168, 174) had been repainted

red to augment the fleet at Sidcup, leaving 13 out of the original 27 still in green livery.

Such was the state of flux at the time with regard to rolling stock that Merton garage lost its 5Q5s on 14th May 1941 to help build up the allocation at Sidcup, only to start receiving others from elsewhere exactly a week later. A particularly difficult capacity problem built up at Harrow Weald whose route 230 was under pressure which could only be relieved by double decking, for which special low height vehicles were required. On 23rd December 1942 four of Harrow Weald's 5Q5s were sent to Merton in exchange for STLs recently fitted at Chiswick with new lowbridge bodywork. An order for 20 bodies was then under construction

The application of safety mesh to windows was a slightly haphazard process which commenced in September 1940 and took a long time to complete, if indeed it was ever fully completed by an overstretched and undermanned engineering staff faced with prioritising numerous other possibly more pressing tasks. Dalston's Q 119's windows were still free of mesh when photographed on 11th June 1943. Its roof has now been repainted from grey to brown but, like all of Dalston's regular 5Q5 fleet, it had not been converted into a standee vehicle. *Alan B Cross*

which turned out to be the last batch of bus bodies to be built by London Transport itself. Further STLs were delivered direct to Harrow Weald as new bodies came off the production line, enabling its last 5Q5 to be released on 1st March 1943.

On Country Buses, Guildford and Dorking retained their 5Q5 allocations throughout the war, but Hatfield's departed on 2nd April 1941 followed by Hertford's on 8th October of the same year. Four of the Hertford contingent moved to Reigate to establish a new 5Q5 outpost there, which also remained in place for the remainder of the war. One of the Reigate vehicles, Q 177, was repainted grey in April 1943 to enable it to work to the Monotype factory in Salfords and remained this way until December 1944 while, surprisingly, Q 175 which had been repainted from green to red in March 1942, reverted to green upon overhaul in February 1944 after working in red livery at Reigate since February 1943

Similarly to the 4Q4s, though not in such great quantity, various 5Q5s were converted to standee format to increase their peak hour carrying potential, in this instance retaining 33 out of their 37 seats to achieve a standing capacity of 20. Sidcup's allocation was treated as top priority for conversion between December 1941 and February 1942, followed by Harrow Weald, Cricklewood, Dorking and Guildford between August and October 1942. When no longer required at Harrow Weald because of double decking, its re-seated 5Q5s moved on initially to Merton and then subsequently to Old Kent Road. In all, 40 5Q5s were converted into standee buses (31 red and 9 green), but none ever worked in this form from Dalston, West Green or Reigate garages which retained conventionally-seated vehicles for their single deck operations..

The war ended with the 80 5Q5s distributed amongst nine garages. Their scheduled Monday to Friday allocation at the start of the 1945 summer programme was:

Garage	Route		Buses scheduled	On books
Cricklewood (W)	226	Golders Green-Cricklewood	6	6
Dalston (D)	208	Clapton-Bromley-by-Bow	5 (plus 6LT)	16
	208A	Clapton-Stratford	10	
Merton (AL)	200	Wimbledon-Coombe Lane	6	7
Old Kent Road (P)	202	Rotherhithe-New Cross	7	7
Sidcup (SP)	241	Sidcup-Welling	17 (plus 3T)	18
West Green (WG)	233	Finsbury Park-Wood Green	11	11
Dorking (DS)	425	Dorking-Guildford	1 (plus 2T)	2
Guildford (GF)	425	Dorking-Guildford	4	8
Reigate (RG)	447	Redhill-South Merstham	5	5
	447A/B	Reigate-South Merstham		

Passenger demand soared in some areas during the wartime years, especially where the need arose to serve factories dedicated to the production of armaments and other war-based demands, and Sidcup's route 241 was one of the first to receive 5Q5s to provide increased carrying capacity. Q 168 was transferred from the Country area on 13th January 1942 and was photographed outside Sidcup garage shortly afterwards being overwhelmed with passengers. Its repaint into red livery had probably been a speedy affair involving only the green areas and leaving the white window frames and grey roof untouched.

The conversion began in December 1941 of 40 5Q5s into 'standee' buses capable of accommodating 53 passengers, not far short of the carrying capacity of many of the smaller double deckers in the fleet such as the STs. Strategically placed stanchions and an array of leather straps were provided for the convenience of standing passengers although the straps may have been inconveniently high and out of reach for many children and some smaller adults. This photograph shows the masks shielding the interior lighting, and window mesh as originally applied with small square holes cut into it to ease visibility before the general adoption of larger, diamond-shaped peepholes with wooden edges This is an early example of the use of the new design of seat moquette subsequently used in huge quantities in post-war years. *London Transport Museum*

The 5Q5s at Sidcup were also scheduled to operate route 228 (Eltham-Chislehurst) on Sundays. At a number of garages the allocation of 5Q5s was 'tight', allowing no spares for maintenance requirements, breakdown or overhauls, all of which were usually covered by miscellaneous T types which were either officially transferred in or borrowed from other garages by local arrangement. Conversely, shortages of other single deck types at Kingston and Sutton garages needed to cover much enhanced Saturday and Sunday operations from 1946 onwards frequently resulted in 5Q5s running from these garages at weekends, usually on loan from Sidcup and most commonly to be found on route 213. In the Country area the 425 schedule was greatly enhanced at weekends to require 7 5Q5s from Guildford on Saturday and 5 on Sunday, with Dorking's allocation doubling to 2 on both days, which explained the seemingly over-generous allocation of 5Q5s at Guildford.

Q 120 was converted with perimeter seating in October 1942 although the altered seating is not visible from outside because of the anti-shatter mesh on the windows. Having worked at a number of other garages beforehand, Q 120 arrived at Old Kent Road in April 1943 and stayed there right through to December 1952. This photograph can be dated to 1944 by the yellow poster above the front wheel seeking men and women conductors. Although the paintwork on Q 120 is quite smart, having been renewed in September 1943, a variety of dents in the panelling hint that the vehicle has led a hard life since then, no doubt exacerbated by the problems of driving safely in the blackout. *W J Haynes*

1945 saw the return to peace, and a concerted effort was made to bring the 5Q5s back into a presentable condition with 32 out of the 80 being presented for overhaul during the year. West Green's Q 114 was dealt with at Chiswick in September 1945 and was photographed on the short-working stand for route 233 at Alexandra Park from where, in pre-war days, single deck trams had entered the private right of way into the grounds of Alexandra Palace. *D W K Jones*

Back in 1945 the 5Q5s were still the newest and most modern large single deckers in the Central Bus fleet, although this was soon to change with the delivery of 81 new T and TD vehicles. However, when they came, the new arrivals were destined not to have any great impact on the Qs which enjoyed a post-war period of comparative stability with no further reallocations to garages at which they had not worked previously. Meanwhile, little time was lost converting the standee vehicles back to conventional seating, a process which commenced in November 1945 and was completed by August 1946 with the exception of a single straggler, Q 158 at Sidcup, which was not dealt with until February 1947.

The biggest impact of the early post-war era, which affected only the red vehicles and not the green ones, was the introduction of a completely revised colour scheme. When the war ended the fleet was in red (or green) with white side window frames, brown roof and black mudguards. With

a very few exceptions the brown roof swept down to waistrail level at the rear, although the three back window frames were usually (but not always) picked out in white. On a few vehicles the brown stopped at the top of the windows allowing white to be applied all the way around the rear at window level, presumably at the whim of whoever was painting the vehicle at the time. The revised Central Bus livery, introduced with the new T and TD vehicles, saw red applied extensively over the body, roof and window frames included, with only the mouldings above and below the windows picked out in a relief colour, which was now cream. When applied to the 5Q5s on overhaul from February 1946 onwards, this certainly succeeded in modernising and improving their appearance although the slow progress of the overhaul programme meant that many red and white specimens continued to found in use right up to 1949. For the record, the last in the old red and white style was Q 168 at Sidcup which went in for overhaul on 31st May 1949. The new style was not applied to the Country vehicles which, in post-war years, retained the green and white colours which they had gained early in the war, but now with grccn roof and mudguards. However this era came to an end in the summer of 1948 as we shall now see.

Between March and September 1948 the Country Bus & Coach department placed into service a small fleet of 30 rather pleasant new Mann Egerton bodied AEC Regals. Known as the 15T13 class, T 769-798 were the first new large single deckers to enter the country fleet for nine years, and though they were all allocated to Hemel

On a few vehicles the white paint surrounding the side windows continued around the back, presumably at the whim of the painter, and this was the case with Merton's Q 108. This vehicle had been overhauled at Chiswick tram depot in April 1945, and when photographed on 24th July 1948 it was beginning to look a little woebegone. It went for its sixth and final overhaul six days later. *Alan B Cross*

The revised livery introduced for red 5Q5s in February 1946 made a big difference to their appearance, and Q 167 is thought to have been the first one to receive it. A Cricklewood-based bus taking a break from its usual work on route 226, it is seen on 31st July 1948 at Wembley on Olympic games duties along with nearly new RT 274 and 18 years old T 16. *V C Jones*

The 'all red' livery, when seen from the back, is demonstrated by Merton's Q 125, which emerged from overhaul in this colour scheme in March 1947. By the time it was photographed on 4th February 1950 the traditional 'white window' livery styling on 5Q5s was a thing of the past. Q 125 was one of the vehicles used for a short period in 1951 to give preliminary training to staff earmarked for driving some of the earliest RFs.
Alan B Cross

In common with so many other single deck classes, 5Q5s occasionally put in an appearance on major in-town routes to cover for the non-availability of double deckers. On this occasion, in October 1948, Cricklewood garage has switched Q 127 to route 16, probably much to the surprise of passengers boarding at Victoria. The division into two of the window behind the driver probably occurred as a glass-saving measure in wartime days.
Alan B Cross

Nearing the end of its days on Country Bus service, Q 164 was photographed in Reigate on 31st May 1948. By this time only 15 out of the original 27 were still green, but not for much longer. Q 164 was destined to be repainted red and sent to Sidcup less than two months later.
Alan B Cross

The last green 5Q5 of all was Q 163 seen picking up passengers at The Fountain, Malden. A Sidcup-based bus, it is operating on loan to Sutton garage – which never had a 5Q5 allocation of its own – on one of the Saturday augmentations which were a feature of the Kingston area single deck services for many years. *Alan B Cross*

Cricklewood's Qs disappeared from route 226 on 14th December 1949 in favour of double deckers. Q 151 worked on it until the end, although latterly in 'all red' livery for the final few months after receiving its last overhaul in August of that year. This was the one and only 1/5Q5/1 on which – although not obvious from this photograph – the back axle was closer to the rear of the vehicle than on the other 79 members of the batch. *D A Jones*

Hempstead and Leavesden Road garages, their arrival inevitably led to widespread reallocations, one of the principal aims of which was to dispose of the 15 5Q5s still operational at Dorking, Guildford and Reigate. All 80 would, at last, be working together in the Central Bus fleet which had been the original intention when the order for them was placed 13 years earlier. At Reigate, the 447 group would be taken over by 4Q4s but, with the latter being banned from operating on route 425, Dorking and Guildford would receive 10T10s as replacements.

A few months ahead of the rest, Q 163 was transferred from Reigate to Sidcup on 13th April 1948, becoming the first 5Q5 to run on Central Buses in green livery. The final day of operation at Reigate and Dorking came on 2nd August with Q 169, 171, 180, 182 passing to Cricklewood the next day, also still in green livery. The situation at Guildford was different. With so many spare 5Q5s for much of the week it was a simple matter to repaint them red, one at a time, during early July, after which seven were added to the Sidcup fleet on the 15th and 16th of the month, leaving only Q 155, 179 at Guildford, both of which had also been repainted red before reaching Sidcup in August. The green ones at Cricklewood were transferred to Sidcup on 2nd September and duly repainted red later that month. Perhaps through an administrative oversight, Q163 remained in service at Sidcup still in green livery right up to 23rd February 1949, on which date it went to Chiswick for its scheduled overhaul from which it emerged in red like all the others.

On 14th December 1949 the number of garages with an allocation of 5Q5s was reduced from six to five when route 226 at Cricklewood went over to double deck operation and its Qs were dispersed to build up the holdings at Dalston, Sidcup and West Green. No further changes of any note took place thereafter, although during 1949 at least 42 members of the batch had their engines converted from indirect to direct injection to improve fuel consumption.

Qs at home, along with a miscellany of other vehicles, in Dalston garage in 1952. Three RTs are present, along with an RTW at the far end which appears to be on driver type-training duties, all of them representing the era of creeping standardisation which had now arrived. Two 5Q5s – the nearest one of which is Q 144 – are also 'at home' as well as an LT single decker. The older double decker, STL 495, is a Hackney garage vehicle probably in for docking. *Ernie Roberts*

Old Kent Road garage had been home to 5Q5s from the very start back in 1936, and when new RFs arrived to replace them in December 1952 five out of the seven then in stock were transferred to finish their last few working weeks at Sidcup and West Green instead of being immediately withdrawn for sale. Q 120 is seen outside Old Kent Road garage and it subsequently went on from there to see further service at Sidcup until the very last day of 5Q5 operation in March 1953. *D A Thompson*

Repainted from green to red in July 1948, Q 173 arrived at Sidcup immediately afterwards and remained there for the rest of its operating career. It received a final overhaul in November 1949 and went on to become one of the very last 5Q5s in revenue service, being one of the final eight withdrawn on 25th March 1953. As was the case with the great majority of 5Q5s, it saw no further use after being sold to W North of Leeds. *Peter Mitchell*

With the arrival of the new RF fleet imminent, five 5Q5s (one from each operating garage) were sent on 31st March 1951 to the training fleet to give drivers at garages scheduled to receive the new buses in the early stages of the programme experience in handling vehicles with a long front overhang. This was, however, only a temporary expedient and all resumed passenger service in April and May.

The last replacement of 5Q5s by new RFs finally began in December 1952 with Merton being dealt with first, then Old Kent Road. West Green and Dalston followed in February 1953, concluding with Sidcup in March. The final withdrawals from service came on 25th March 1953 when Q 139 was delicensed at Dalston and Q 131 at West Green, both having been retained up to then alongside the new RFs as engineers' spares, together with Q 120, 165, 168, 173, 176, 178 at Sidcup. After a few months in storage at a variety of bus and trolleybus depots, and also at the Walthamstow yard and in the Kingsway tram subway, all were sold to W North of Leeds between March 1953 and April 1954.

With their open entrance ahead of the front wheels designed to such a shape that fitment of a front door was virtually impossible, it is small wonder that, despite its sales expertise, North's found no home for the 5Q5s within the UK, not even for humble uses such as store sheds and mobile caravans. However, a few were exported, the most well documented examples being to Libya where they worked in Tripoli alongside 4Q4s, with Q 137, 142 and 184 in the fleet of Guiseppi Cavazzini and Q 153 with the CIFLA company. All had the driver's position and entrance doorway transposed to suit the rule of the road. Q 158 and 182 are known to have operated in Cyprus while Q 145, 168, 169, 172 saw further service in virtually unaltered condition in the Burmese capital, Rangoon.

Comparatively few 5Q5s saw service after their London Transport days and this vehicle was a rarity in being converted to left hand drive with the revised entrance door replicating fairly closely the original, albeit in reverse. This unidentified vehicle was seen in 1956 in the yard of Guiseppe Cavazzini in Tripoli, Libya, along with a pair of Fiats. *Brian Parnell*

North's of Leeds offered Qs for sale to overseas operators at £450 each. Two 5Q5s are known to have gone to Cyprus, although there might well have been more, and this one has yet to be identified. With Cyprus following the same rule of the road as the UK there was no need for any modification, apart from a change of livery, for this vehicle to take an active role in the Famagusta Bus Service fleet. *David Ruddom*

Newly built Q 197 is seen in a coachbuilder's photograph before receiving its registration plates. Destination blind material and side route boards have been supplied as part of Park Royal's contract but the lettering will be applied to them by London Transport after arrival at Chiswick. Park Royal's well-known 'sedan chair' transfer can be seen at the foot of the front mudguard, and another one is placed in the same position on the offside. *Park Royal Coachworks*

GREEN LINE COACHES Q 189 – Q 238

For the first fifteen months of its existence the main focus of the new London Passenger Transport Board with regard to its newly inherited bus and coach fleet had been to establish some sort of cohesion amongst the incredibly mixed bag of vehicles that it had inherited and to establish a credible programme of replacing the older and more exotic ones amongst them. Initial attention had focussed on procuring new buses as distinct from coaches, but by October 1934 Chief Engineer A A M Durrant was able to announce that steps were being taken to complete a suitable design

for Green Line work on the assumption that such vehicles would be four-wheelers of 27ft 6ins length. In truth, new rolling stock was desperately needed on the Green Line network which, though marketed as a premium service, was coming in for heavy criticism for being worked entirely by what were perceived as old-fashioned vehicles well past their prime. In addition, there was a desire by the engineers to remove as quickly as possible the large number of Gilfords, which were temperamental and expensive to maintain, of which no fewer than 114 were employed regularly on Green Line work.

By February 1935 an outline for a new coach had been drawn up. Once again it was based on the AEC Q chassis which had now been adopted as the Board's preferred single decker for new deliveries, and it followed the general layout of the 4Q4 with short front and rear overhangs of 4ft 0½ ins and 4ft 10½ ins respectively and a long wheelbase of 18ft 6ins, on which the entrance was placed immediately behind the front wheel facing a longitudinal seat over the engine compartment. On 7th June 1935 Frank Pick directed that a programme for 100 new coaches "or such number as may be found necessary" should be drawn up as soon as possible with the aim of them all being in service by March 1936. A week later the final drawings for the bodywork were approved, and the decision was taken to issue tenders for 100 metal framed bodies to the MCW organisation and to BRCW. It is presumed that BRCW declined to tender and the offer was subsequently extended to Park Royal instead.

Tenders were duly received and it was decided that, to expedite delivery, 50 bodies would be allocated to Park Royal and the other 50 identical ones to the MCW affiliate company, Weymann. Meanwhile, midway through the tendering process, London Transport complicated the process by modifying its body design in a number of ways, and most noticeably by eliminating a pair of seats at the very front of the nearside facing the driver and inserting instead a full-width bulkhead, thereby acknowledging the serious problems then being encountered on the 4Q4s but reducing the seating capacity to 32. The rake in the roofline, which had been a feature on the 4Q4s and 5Q5s, was now eliminated. Chiswick's body design incorporated what was called a 'power' ventilation system producing warm air throughout the passenger saloon in colder months and cool air in the summer, and by early in January 1936 it had become clear that work on this aspect of the design would not be completed in time

Q 195 has been fully fitted out for operation on route M3 in readiness for its official London Transport photos to be taken, even to the extent of providing a "1d fares on this coach" slip board at the foot of the nearside windscreen. The plain, square-edged air vents fitted to the 6Q6s below the registration plate were destined to last only a short time before being replaced by more stylish ones similar to those on the 5Q5s. Q 195 entered service at Guildford on 14th November 1936.
London Transport Museum

London Transport's current standards in regard to décor and general internal fitments for the Green Line fleet had already been established with the 9T9s which preceded the 6Q6s into service by five months, and the only real difference between the two lay in the provision on the latter of eight inward-facing seats to cover the engine and front wheel arches, a feature which never gained popular acceptance on Green Line work. *Park Royal Coachworks*

to achieve the desired March delivery target. A number of high level meetings took place to resolve the situation, and it was finally decided that one half of the order should be switched to AEC Regals (on which AEC could promise quick delivery), reducing the Q content to 50 with a hoped-for delivery date of August for the first complete coach. Park Royal would retain its contract for the Qs while Weymann would produce what became known as the 9T9 class (T404-453). An order for all of these was duly authorised on 30th January 1936 at a total cost of £200,250 (£100,750 for the Qs and £99,500 for the Ts).

It is interesting to record that this episode

marked the sudden end of London Transport's short-lived addiction to the AEC Q. Frank Pick had been involved in the restructuring of the contract resulting in the unplanned acquisition of 50 AEC Regals, and had expressed the view that, having regard to the unfavourable arrangement of seats in Q-type vehicles (longitudinal seats being particularly unsuitable on longer distance work) it might be desirable to adopt the T type for further new coaches when these were required. This effectively rang the death knell for the Q which AEC had struggled to sell to operators other than London Transport. So low was the demand for it that, after the production of the last

5Q5 with chassis number 0762261, a subsequent batch of 25 chassis numbers had been set aside for provincial or overseas buyers of which only eight had been built. The 6Q6s, as the new Green Line coaches became known, occupied chassis numbers 0762287-336 and these marked the end of the line.

The fifty 6Q6s were allocated fleet numbers Q 189-238 with body numbers 16730-16779, and were registered CXX 382-406/DGX 220-244. The intermediate fleet number Q 188 was reserved for a six-wheeled double deck coach (described later) which, though ordered before the 6Q6s, was delivered after them. The first chassis from the AEC production line was Q 189 which went to Park Royal on 24th June 1936, and the fully completed vehicle arrived at Chiswick in time to undergo intensive testing between 1st and 3rd October. There was no immediate entry into service because it was found to be overweight as a result of modifications requested by London Transport, principally the partition behind the driver, requiring the first ten completed vehicles to be modified to comply with MOT requirements. It was not until 3rd November that the first 6Q6 was licensed for service (Q 200 at Guildford), long after the end of the summer operating season for which they had originally been required.

Although the Chiswick draughtsmen had done their best to produce a modern and eye-catching design, the 6Q6 always looked a little ungainly and awkward, in stark contrast to Chiswick's later harmonious designs for the 10T10 and TF Green Line coaches. The stipulation of a high and completely flat floor with ample internal headroom produced an overall unladen height of 10ft 3¼ins which, with the vehicle's chunky frontal appearance and abbreviated rear end, gave it a rather squat and ungainly air. The outside was finished in the then-current shade of mid-green with lighter green side window surrounds, the two shades being separated by thin black mouldings, with mudguards also picked out in

Hertford-based Q 205 makes a stop in Hoddesdon as it heads north on route M2 from West Byfleet back to its home town. Although still showing all the gloss of newness, the polished metal surrounds to the front registration plate and air intake have already been covered by a coat of green paint in what appears to have been a policy decision to disguise them for some unknown reason. *J F Higham © A B Cross*

It was fortuitous that London Transport's photographer secured this shot of Hertford's Q 217 as it passed Marble Arch in February 1937 on its way to Byfleet, very lightly loaded and with its conductor apparently enjoying a breath of fresh air through the partly-open door. Q 217 was destined to be the only one of London Transport's single deck Qs not to survive the war intact. *London Transport Museum*

black. A neat arrangement at the front combined the air intake panel of the heating system with the registration plate inside a polished grille, but the latter was unfortunately soon rendered less effective by being painted over.

Internally the standard Green Line décor consisting mainly of shades of green with cream ceiling and luggage rack panels, which had been introduced on the 9T9s, was now perpetuated on the Qs. The biggest drawback of the vehicles was the predominance of inward-facing seats at

the front consisting of two on the nearside ahead of the doorway and four on the offside over the engine. Service experience soon showed that these were generally unpopular and were usually the ones that were occupied last, the seven nearside and six offside transverse pairs normally being the seats of choice for longer journeys. In common with the 4Q4s before them, the main entry door to the driver's cab was on the offside of the vehicle and, like the 5Q5s, their emergency door was at the back.

Park Royal's 'sedan chair' transfer is still clearly visible on Q 228 although the paintwork has now lost its shine. Interestingly, a sheet of what appears to be a canvas-like material has been fairly roughly attached over the bottom air intake grille and painted to match the main body colour. The side-mounted board for the M group of services incorporates supplementary holders for the route number and southern terminus descriptor to avoid the cumbersome process of having to remove the heavy main board when vehicles swap from one route to another. *J F Higham © A B Cross*

The overall mechanical specification for the 6Q6s was virtually the same as the two previous batches which, in common with those and all other Qs ever built, required the air pressure in the offside tyres to be set at a notably higher level than on the nearside to counter the sheer imbalance of weight inherent in the side engine design. Powered by the standard 7.7 engine, and with the same axle ratio (5.4:1) as the other two batches but weighing much more, the 6Q6s were hardly speedy performers and would have encountered difficulty in adhering to the fast timings on many Green Line services. At a prodigious 6 tons 13cwt 1qr (later amended to 6-15-0) they weighed in at just over a ton heavier than the 4Q4s and about half a ton more than the 5Q5s.

All 50 6Q6s were overhauled during 1938 resulting from which they appeared in the latest Green Line livery with Lincoln green as the main colour and a thin bronze line instead of dark green on the horizontal mouldings separating the two shades of green. The windscreen surrounds were no longer picked out in the darker colour. Q 235, an Amersham-based vehicle, is on a short-working journey to Uxbridge and shares the stand with all-Leyland F1 class trolleybus 660 which was taken into stock in April 1937 and is just four months Q 235's junior.

After an early spell at Hammersmith, Q 226 spent most of the war – from May 1940 onwards – based at Chalk Farm, where it stayed until it ceased to be an ambulance on 1st May 1946. For most of the war it remained in the Green Line colours received on overhaul in September 1938, getting ever more dowdy through being kept permanently in the open. With full blackout lamp masking, it stands in front of TF 26 which has been repainted at some time during the war into green and white bus colours. The later photograph, taken in the company of a 9T9 after blackout restrictions were lifted, finds Q 226 fully repainted into green and white but still carrying GREEN LINE fleet names. *S A Newman © A B Cross*

The M group of Green Line services was the first to be selected for operation by the new Qs (M1 Hertford-Guildford, M2 Hertford-Byfleet, M3 Hertford-Esher). Guildford garage was stocked first starting with Q 200 and Q 206 on 3rd November 1936, followed by Hertford and then Addlestone, with the whole operation completed by 17th December. Next came Luton in late December 1936 and early January 1937 for route H3 (Luton-Kings Cross), followed also in January by High Wycombe for route Q (High Wycombe-Oxford Circus) and finally Amersham for route R (Chesham-Oxford Circus). The latter was only a part conversion to use up the residue of Qs, other scheduled rolling stock on it being mainly 9T9s but also one older petrol T-type. Of the 50 6Q6s, 43 were scheduled for service on Sundays to Fridays rising to 45 on Saturdays.

Not all went completely smoothly with the 6Q6s at first. As with the 5Q5s, the floor bars on their Park Royal bodies were soon found to need strengthening, resulting in all 50 vehicles being returned to their builder, one at a time, between 21st May and 6th October 1937. The saloon heating system was quite quickly found to be less effective than had been hoped, and the five outlets along each side of the vehicle at floor level, though theoretically adequate, were often found to be ineffective although more than a decade was to elapse before a lasting remedy was found for this. Much quicker action was taken over drivers' complaints of poor road holding and skidding, with Q 236 despatched to Fort Dunlop in Birmingham between 30th August and 6th September 1937 (accompanied by a 9T9, T 405, for comparison purposes) for extensive skidding tests as recorded earlier under the 5Q5 heading.

With declaration of war expected imminently the whole Green Line network was withdrawn on 1st September 1939, and within two days all fifty 6Q6s had been converted into emergency ambulances capable of carrying six seated passengers on the existing longitudinal seats, plus eight stretchers. In this form they were distributed to a wide variety of garages throughout the London Transport fleet to wait emergency call-outs and to

Q 234 was one of the first 6Q6s to re-enter service after a 6½ year gap, on 1st March 1946. One of five allocated to Crawley garage and photographed at the Baker Street terminus of route 710, it was newly repainted into the green and white colour scheme. The conductor looks happy enough, but these coaches were not liked by staff and within three months Q 234 had moved to a more permanent home at Guildford. The paper notice adjacent to the door reads "Courtesy Aids Service". *S A Newman © A B Cross*

assist in transferring patients between hospitals. The whole batch was absent from the London passenger transport scene for the entire six years of the war, and it was not until October 1945 that any were released from ambulance work.

Although many were kept at vulnerable locations as ambulances, the only wartime casualty amongst the class occurred on the evening of 18th July 1944 when a German V1 rocket hit Elmers End garage. The bodywork of Q 217 was extensively damaged, and at the direction of the Ministry of War Transport the vehicle was conveyed to Northern Coachbuilders on 31st August 1944 for construction of a new body at their wartime works in an old aircraft hangar at Cramlington in Northumberland. Although much of the framework for a new body was machined it was never assembled, and Q 217's chassis was sent back to Chiswick on 19th June 1945 with all the new parts loaded on it. A decision was taken on 9th August to erect the new body at Chiswick "when circumstances permit" at a cost of about £1,000 using the parts provided by Northern Coachbuilders, but this decision was subsequently

rescinded. In February 1946 the conclusion was reached that construction of the body was neither economical nor feasible under existing circumstances and soon afterwards, on 29th March, Q 217 was written off books, its chassis having been dismantled at Chiswick for spares.

Between 24th October 1945 and 25th May 1946 39 out of the remaining 49 6Q6s were released by the health authorities and converted at Chiswick back for coach operation, these now being the oldest vehicles in the Green Line fleet. It was deemed necessary to keep a few on as ambulances with three (Q 192, 199, 208) still fulfilling this role as late into the post-war era as 1948. The last coach ambulance of all, Q 192, was delicensed at Hackney garage on 8th July of that year. Meanwhile, with most of them looking quite scruffy at the war's end, having not been overhauled since 1938, a repainting programme got under way from the end of 1945 onwards to improve their external appearance ready for the resumption of Green Line duties. Initially the wartime livery of Lincoln green with white around the window on the sides and back was applied, albeit with a green roof

Route 714 commenced on 29th May 1946 and was never officially a 6Q6 operation. Q 237 was photographed at Victoria on 2nd June, the day after it was officially transferred from Crawley to Guildford although, as the photograph shows, it was actually running on loan to Dorking at the time deputising for a TF. This vehicle also carries the green and white colour scheme under which, in nearly all cases, the back window area was picked out in white as shown here. The new post-war Green Line blind arrangement of black lettering on an amber background has now come into use. *S A Newman © A B Cross*

to replace the brown that had been applied as a wartime camouflage measure, and as many as 24 were repainted in this manner. From April 1946 onwards the full post-war two-tone green Green Line livery was used, even being applied to those vehicles still in use as ambulances. However, a concerted overhaul programme introduced in March 1947 meant that all of them received yet another coat of paint, and by April 1948 the green and white style had been eliminated from the 6Q6 fleet.

Post-war Green Line operation commenced on 6th February 1946 with the introduction of route 715, but the reinvigorated 6Q6s did not appear on the scene until 1st March when Godstone garage received six for route 709 (Caterham-Baker Street) and Crawley was allocated five for the 710 (Crawley-Baker Street) ready to start operation on the 6th. On 3rd April it was the turn of Reigate to commence route 711 (Reigate-Baker Street) with Qs and for High Wycombe to start route 724 (High Wycombe-Oxford Circus). Finally came Amersham on 19th June with Green Line operation of route 725 (Chesham-Baker Street). Thirty-three 6Q6s

were now licensed for passenger service from five garages, only two of which were ones from which they had operated in pre-war years. Operating staff at the other three were not happy with the Qs whose performance in respect of speed and agility compared poorly with the more powerful 10T10s to which they had become accustomed in pre-war times. The obvious solution was to return the Qs back to where they had operated most effectively in the past, the former M group of routes now simplified into the 715 (Hertford-Guildford). In an overnight exchange of rolling stock, the Qs left Godstone, Crawley and Reigate and took up service at Hertford and Guildford garages on 1st June 1946 from which they operated efficiently right through to the RF era in 1952.

Meanwhile, general dissatisfaction with the performance of the 6Q6s as Green Line coaches permeated to Amersham and High Wycombe garages and these, too, were turned over to 10T10 operation in November 1947. It was now fully accepted by London Transport that finding further Green Line work for them was out of the question, but staff representatives agreed to accept their

Route 715 eventually became the sole Green Line service on which 6Q6s could regularly be found with a daily allocation of 21 vehicles (10 from Guildford and 11 from Hertford) to cater for its 20 minute frequency. During the course of a typical day's operation Q 214 has returned to Hertford garage to facilitate a crew changeover. Photographed at an unknown date, it has now lost its semaphore trafficators and also the offside one of its two cab ventilators. *D A Thompson*

The 6Q6s were the oldest and lowest powered coaches scheduled for Green Line work after the war and the only route which they seemed to cope with comfortably was the Hertford to Guildford 715, probably because its end-to-end timings were arranged to suit their less than spectacular performance. On this occasion the vehicle is Guildford-based Q 209 which served the 715 well until its withdrawal on 1st January 1952.

A largely forgotten part of London Transport history is that a few single deckers remained in use as ambulances well into the post-war era. They included Q 208 which continued to be based for this purpose at Chelverton Road until as late as 5th July 1948, more than three years after the war in Europe had ceased. In the meantime it had been repainted into current post-war Green Line livery and thus needed little external work to return it to service at Hertford on 1st October 1948. The letters EMS on the yellow triangle stand for 'Emergency Medical Service'.

redeployment on bus services within the Country area. The garages selected for this were Guildford, which was in any case already well familiar with the 6Q6s and received all of the former High Wycombe fleet on 12th November, and St Albans which took in the 6Q6s from Amersham on the same date. Although quite a high proportion of the 6Q6 fleet was now employed as buses, the whole batch of 49 remained officially classified as coaches, retaining the C suffix to their fleet numbers accordingly.

Although they were now approaching old age, a few improvements were carried out on the 6Q6s between 1948 and 1950 in an endeavour to improve conditions for passengers and staff. The efficiency of their heating systems had long been unpredictable, and a series of internal plates was inserted at the ventilator apertures with the aim of ensuring that warm air was directed into the main part of the body instead of being lost between the outer and inner panels. To improve matters further by eliminating uncomfortable draughts, the ventilators above each windscreen (which had seldom been used by drivers in post-war years) were covered over with plates riveted on the outside of the bodywork. Further modifications carried out included removal of the now-disused semaphore trafficators, whose apertures were plated over, and the strengthening of the pillars holding the emergency doors which were beginning to flex with age and tending to fly open when vehicles were in motion.

1951 was destined to be the last full year of 6Q6 operation, and at the end of the year the class was distributed fairly evenly among the three garages with 18 at Hertford, 16 at Guildford and 15 at St Albans. On 1st January 1952 withdrawals commenced in earnest with new RF coaches taking over Green Line operations during the month, first at Hertford and then at Guildford. At the same time St. Albans' Qs were all swept away by an influx of TFs displaced from the 723/A at Grays and now demoted to bus status. The last 6Q6 left St. Albans on 1st February but a few managed to hang on at Hertford, mainly on Green Line duplication work, until the last one left on 12th March, while Guildford's final three survived until 13th April. A few were allocated to trainer duties, but for most it looked very much as though the end was nigh, until an unusual occurrence took place.

Q 202, now minus both cab ventilators, worked regularly on a variety of St Albans bus services between November 1947 and December 1951 despite optimistically continuing to carry GREEN LINE fleet names. It is seen on 27th March 1948 laying over at the garage between duties alongside AEC Regal UR 6895 on hire from the Premier Omnibus Company of Watford for peak hour work on route 330. *Alan B Cross*

St Albans' 6Q6s occasionally returned to Green Line relief work to back up the regular TFs on routes 712 and 713, especially on Sundays when two duplicates were regularly scheduled alongside the normal allocation of seven. In this instance Q 213 appears to be gathering a full load at Victoria for its return run to St Albans. Its running number, SA 104, indicates that at least four duplicates are in action on this particular Monday, 6th June 1949. *Alan B Cross*

In the Central area, the driving staff at Muswell Hill garage had become restless about having to drive LT class 'Scooter' single deckers dating from 1931 and were agitating for them to be replaced urgently. Although these six-wheelers were undoubtedly old fashioned in appearance most were, in fact, in good condition for their age having been substantially rebuilt with virtually new bodywork as recently as 1948/49. The problem at Muswell Hill lay more with their performance than their age. In 1950 they had received AEC 7.7 oil engines taken from withdrawn STLs in place of their petrol units, and herein lay the problem. In petrol engine days Muswell Hill's LT single deckers had always been fitted with more powerful engines than those elsewhere in the fleet to help them cope with the tortuous local terrain which included the steep Highgate Hill and the even more testing Muswell Hill. This same power differential had not been maintained when the vehicles were converted to oilers, and they undoubtedly struggled badly on the hills as a result of this. The staff had become aware that the 6Q6s had become surplus to requirements and asked to have some in replacement for LTs. Even after it was pointed out that the 6Q6s were similarly powered to the LTs and would perform no better than them, and also that brand new RFs were scheduled at Muswell Hill garage as early as October 1952, the drivers remained insistent. On the understanding that no special work would be carried out on the Qs and that they would remain in green livery, the request was agreed to.

The first four 6Q6s arrived at Muswell Hill on 1st March 1952 and full scale operation of the type commenced on the 19th. Individual vehicles came and went according to their mechanical condition and certificate of fitness expiries, but the regular number of operational vehicles stabilised at 19. This was enough to cover scheduled requirements on routes 210 (Finsbury Park-Golders Green) and 244 (Muswell Hill-Winchmore Hill), but vehicle allocations at Muswell Hill were always quite flexible and appearances were quite often recorded on the short but very busy 212 (Muswell Hill-Finsbury Park) with its maximum peak hour schedule of no fewer than 46 buses per hour. The only outward difference made to the vehicles from Country Bus days was the application of the LONDON TRANSPORT fleet name instead of GREEN LINE, and for the first time in their lives advertising matter appeared on the backs of them. As predicted, new RFs began to arrive at Muswell Hill in September, scheduled for route 212 but

The arrival of 6Q6s on Central Bus work at Muswell Hill caused great excitement for the enthusiast fraternity of the day and certainly marked a very unusual twist of fate for the class at the very tail end of its service career. The 210 was the best route on which to find them and it had the added interest of serving a great diversity of operating terrain. Q 235 is seen in North End Way loading and unloading passengers for Hampstead Heath while Q 194 is in busy surroundings at Archway along with three trolleybuses on route 611, including J3 class 1047, and also class E3 tram 1986 on the final day of operation of the Kingsway Subway services on 5th April 1952. Q 194 only lasted at Muswell Hill until the end of May but Q 235 survived until mid-September.
E J Smith / Alan B Cross

Fully laden, Q 204 sets out from Golders Green on yet another busy run to Finsbury Park. The bodywork on the 6Q6s always looked rather low at the rear, potential grounding not being a particular source of worry with such a short rear overhang, but the back springs look extra-weak on this particular vehicle. For the first time in their lives the 6Q6s at Muswell Hill carried commercial advertising on the back panels. Allan T Smith © A B Cross

releasing TDs to replace the Qs and enabling withdrawal of the latter to begin on the 10th of the month. By the end of September only ten Qs remained, reducing to five by the end of October. The final 6Q6 in passenger service, and fittingly the highest numbered one, Q 238, was delicensed on 11th December 1952 bringing the 6Q6 chapter on London Transport nearly to a close. A solitary vehicle, Q 216, remained licensed for a few days into 1953, ostensibly as a trainer, but this was withdrawn on 14th January bringing London Transport's association with the 6Q6s to an end.

Sales proceeded steadily between February and October 1953 with a single survivor, Q 233, disposed of in February 1954 once it had been confirmed that it would not be required for the preserved fleet. Almost all went to W North of Leeds who passed the great majority on to breakers, there being little further demand for them. Despite its expertise in procuring overseas customers, North's is known to have sold only two abroad, both to the Gold Coast, while two others remained within the UK converted into racing car transporters.

Apart from route 210, the other service on which 6Q6s could regularly be found during their short spell at Muswell Hill was the 244, a quieter and much less taxing operation. At the Muswell Hill Broadway terminus on 25th June 1952 Q 211 shares operation of the 244 with a vehicle of a vastly different type, 1947-built Leyland PS1 TD 26. Q 211 stayed in service at Muswell Hill until 29th October 1952. Alan B Cross

Surprising vehicles sometimes turned up on Kingston area services on Saturdays but probably none more so than Q 216 which was found working route 213 from Kingston garage on Saturday 10th May 1952 on what may well have been the first and last time a 6Q6 ran on a Central Bus service, other than latterly at Muswell Hill. Standing alongside it is T 719, of the 'regulars' on the 213. Officially a training vehicle based at far-off Potters Bar, Q 216's real function in life at this time is not really known, but it remained in use longer than all the other vehicles of its type and was still officially working as a trainer into the start of 1953. *Ken Blacker*

The scrap man awaits! With virtually no future demand for their services, Qs 195, 193, 190 and 226 make a depressing sight as they stand for some eighteen months, unused and unwanted, in the yard of Guildford garage. All were sold to W North of Leeds in the second half of 1953 and were never heard of again. *Michael Rooum*

By the time that Q 188 saw the light of day in March 1937 large, sleek six-wheeled double deckers were already becoming commonplace in trolleybus form, but this was undoubtedly one of the most impressive and modern-looking diesel double deckers ever built in pre-war years. The long side windows, with many grouped unusually into pairs on the upper deck, plus other interesting design features such as the gentle curve at the foot of the upstairs front windows and the slight outward flair at the foot of many of the lower deck panels, all added to its sleek ultra-modern appearance. It seems odd that, with such a prestigious vehicle, the Chiswick authorities did not take the trouble to fit its polished front wheel nut guards before posing it on Ham Common for its official photographs. *London Transport Museum*

DOUBLE DECK COACH Q 188

The last to be dealt with in this volume is Q 188, a vehicle which has gone down in the annals of Green Line history as a worthy but unsuccessful attempt to create a suitable double deck equivalent to the traditional single deck Green Line coach. The benefit of having such vehicles in the fleet was obvious. There were many services on the Green Line network where double deckers could prove financially advantageous, especially at busy periods when the necessity to operate a considerable number of costly duplications could be avoided. Green Line was marketed as a premium service, with fares to match, and any suitable double decker needed to be a clear cut improvement over the run-of-the-mill double deck bus, which Q 188 aimed to be.

The concept of a high-capacity, six-wheeled oil-engined double decker with offside engine and transmission was not a completely new one. As far back as July 1933, the very first month of the LPTB's existence, Lord Ashfield had approved the construction of just such a vehicle for experimental purposes, and drawings for it were prepared. Although the project did not go ahead at the time for reasons now unknown, the concept clearly did not die but was re-born a few years later in Q 188.

Q 188 marked the second attempt to create an extra-special double decker specifically for Green Line work, the previous project having taken place prior to the LPTB era, in 1931, with the strikingly unusual-looking LT 1137. For a variety of reasons this had ultimately failed in its mission to establish a role for double deckers on Green Line, having achieved little more than two years' operation before the experiment was brought to a halt and the vehicle was demoted to bus work. With this

The offside view gives an idea of how the vehicle would have looked in Green Line service with a route board in place.
London Transport Museum

experience still fairly fresh in the minds of the Chiswick development and design staff, the way was clear with Q 188 to learn from the errors and avoid the pitfalls that had brought LT 1137's coach career to such an abrupt and premature end.

The exact circumstances leading up to the design and development of Q 188 featuring a Q-type chassis and Park Royal bodywork are not known, but formal approval for the vehicle to be ordered was given in July 1935. The expenditure authorised for it was a hefty £3,500 which would have covered design as well as manufacturing

Very few photos are known to have been taken of Q 188 on service in London, and those that exist were all taken during its one-year-long spell of activity from Hertford garage. This view is at the Hertford North terminus of the 313 where the conductor can be seen at the upstairs front changing the destination display. Although Q 188's bulk makes it appear to be a powerful machine, looks in this case are deceptive.
D Evans © Omnibus Society

costs. There must have been considerable to-ing and fro-ing between the design teams at Chiswick and the manufacturers' representatives at AEC and Park Royal, as both chassis and body were complete one-offs totally unlike anything else on either company's production line. The chassis, in particular, was unique in being the only Q ever manufactured to a three-axle layout, in which form it received its unique AEC type classification 0763 with chassis number 0763001.

Although they looked entirely different, Q 188 and LT 1137 in fact had several major features in common, notably in that both were six wheelers with both rear axles driven, but for manoeuvrability reasons were shorter than the maximum permitted length for this type of vehicle (Q 188 was 27ft 6ins long and LT 1137 28ft 7½ ins). Both had their passenger entrance sited at the forward end of the vehicle just behind the front wheel, and both had a low seating capacity relative to their size (51 seats in Q 188 and 50 in LT 1137) to provide maximum legroom and comfort for long distance travellers. Q 188 did not perpetuate the example set by LT 1137 in having an opening roof on the top deck, nor did it try to achieve the ultra-low height of the LT (14ft 0ins), being a more comfortable 14ft 4½ ins.

The contract for the chassis of Q 188 was placed soon after the order for the two additional 4Q4s (Q 186, 187) was confirmed in November 1935, and it was logical for its fleet number to follow on immediately after these. Its body number, 16130, was in fact lower than these two and of the 5Q5s. The completed chassis was delivered to Chiswick on 19th May 1936, presumably for inspection, before being despatched to Park Royal. The latter took a full half year constructing the body, enabling the complete vehicle to be delivered to Chiswick on 1st February 1937 by which time even the 6Q6s had been in service for more than six months. Q 188 was classified 7Q7, and at last the 238-strong Q class was complete.

The interior of Q 188 replicated the décor and general fittings in the 9T9s and 6Q6s but lacked luggage racks. For a vehicle intended for longish journeys the forward view from the lower saloon was disappointing. The staircase blocked the view of the road ahead from its offside seats while, on the nearside, the seats closest to the front faced inwards towards the staircase, providing the passengers sitting in them with hardly any outward vision at all. Closest to the camera are the single seats adjacent to the rear wheel arches. *London Transport Museum*

The high level of flair and innovation that had gone into designing the exterior of Q 188 to produce something eye-catching and out of the ordinary was not replicated inside the vehicle. The lack of internal luggage racks, and the absence of any compensating adornments at ceiling level, rendered the interior very `bus-like' in appearance. This was particularly noticeable looking towards the rear on the upper deck which did not look so very different from the contemporary front-entrance Country area STL service bus. Even the luggage rack provided at the top of the stairs was a surprisingly modest affair which lacked depth and was not even provided with rails to prevent items from falling off when cornering. *London Transport Museum*

Q 188 looked like no other vehicle on London Transport. In typical Q format its back wheels were placed close to the rear corners but thanks to having a four-wheel back bogie the whole ensemble looked much better balanced than was normally the case with Q-type vehicles. Due to having an additional axle, the wheelbase was reduced to 16ft 10½ins, the bogie wheelbase being exactly 4ft. A side product of having four wheels at the back would have been that the Q's normal propensity for poor road holding and skidding was very much reduced, but on the other hand the chances of getting much speed out of the vehicle would have been minimal as it was fitted only with the customary 7.7 oil engine which, with an official unladen weight of 9tons 0cwt 0qr, gave an uncomfortably poor power-to-weight ratio. In many respects, Q 188's technical specification

reflected that of the other Q-type oilers in the fleet except in the case of the gearbox. Fitted at London Transport's specific request as something of an afterthought, and probably prompted by the fact that identical units were being used successfully on urban buses in Paris, it was a French-designed Cotal unit which used electro-magnets in place of brakes operated by springs or hydraulic pressure to control the various elements in the epicyclic mechanism. Bean Industries manufactured the Cotal gearbox under licence in the UK and it was probably purchased from them.

The body on Q 188 was striking in appearance and extremely modern for its time, with a front end that was even more raked than the earlier double deck Qs and with wide side windows which, on the upper deck, were unusually grouped in pairs, each with a narrow, black painted intermediate pillar. The windows were mounted in metal pans with rounded corners, and inside the passenger saloons they were capped by shaped metal shrouds identical to those favoured by London Transport for single deckers but never applied to double deckers (with the sole exception of this vehicle) until the arrival of the RTs. The internal fittings and décor were completely in line with current Green Line practice, but the seating layout was, of course, unique. The staircase, which faced the sliding entrance door, was mounted over the engine compartment, eliminating the unpopular bench seats normally placed in this position, but inward-facing seats were not entirely absent from the lower saloon as a group of three was placed on the nearside forward of the doorway over the front wheel arch. Further back in the saloon, two single seats were placed on each side adjacent to the long rear wheel arches, and the total seating capacity downstairs was only 23. On the upper deck all 28 seats were forward facing. Q 188 suffered from the same drawback as LT 1137 in having no overhead luggage racks, and once again luggage storage space was in short supply which would be a major drawback on services where a high percentage of passengers carried suitcases or other items of luggage.

Q 188 was attractively painted in the standard two tone green livery outlined in an even darker green, but it also had a silver roof and was the only modern Green Line vehicle to do so. It was unusual in that, at the front, the silver swept down to encompass the front windows while, at the back, the whole of the dome and emergency window surrounds were in green. An unusual new three-piece indicator box layout was introduced at both front and rear. Top and bottom boxes, which were comparatively shallow, carried the destination details and a GREEN LINE legend respectively, while the much deeper central box was used to show the main via points. Mountings for conventional wooden route boards were provided on each side just above the lower deck windows.

The new vehicle stayed at Chiswick for only a few weeks before it went back to AEC on 24th March 1937, returning from there almost three months later on 10th June. This purpose of this long visit to the chassis maker is not known, but it may have been to install and test the Cotal gearbox. Intensive testing, and perhaps further modification work, then took place at Chiswick before the vehicle was finally licensed as DGO 500 and delivered to the Country Bus & Coach department at Reigate on 6th September 1937. Once again, information on its activities while at Reigate is sparse, and London Transport remained remarkably reticent and publicity-shy on the matter. Clearly, exhaustive out-of-service test running over Green Line routes would have taken place, but there is no evidence that Q 188 ever operated in public service as a Green Line coach. It is known that the Reigate management was dissatisfied with its performance, and especially its lack of adequate power and frequent overheating, and rumour has it that the operating staff's union representatives refused to allow it on Green Line work because of these inadequacies.

Just over six weeks later, on 22nd October, Q 188 was sent back to Chiswick to await its fate. The fitting of a larger, more powerful engine was found to be out of the question because space could not be made within the structure to accommodate one, and in due course the decision was taken to abandon any hope of getting the vehicle into a fit condition to run on the Green Line network. The management decided to cut its losses and find a niche for Q 188 as a service bus. It had been an intriguing and imaginative design exercise but had proved to be an even bigger failure as a Green Line coach than LT 1137. To make matters worse its cost had spiralled above budget by a massive £893, a 25% over-run, thought largely to be due to the belated decision to install the Cotal gearbox.

On 1st June 1938 Q 188 was sent to Hertford garage where it was subsequently joined by the other double deck Qs on bus route 310. Its demotion to bus duties was accompanied by amending the fleet numbers to read Q 188B instead of Q 188C and by replacing the GREEN LINE names with LONDON TRANSPORT. Apart from painting over the glass on the bottom destination screens to eliminate the GREEN LINE inscription nothing else appears to have been done to Q 188 to prepare it for its new career. After some months at Hertford

In Hoddesdon's wide High Street, Q 188 makes its way towards Enfield in wintry surroundings. Nowadays the roadway at this point is narrow and an ugly and unsympathetic tower block spoils the view. Since the previous photograph of it on service was taken a destination blind showing the route number and destination, of the type used on STs, has been placed in the centre box, and presumably the narrow top display has fallen into disuse although the build-up of snow makes this unclear. *Mick Webber collection*

it was fitted – as were certain of the other double deck Qs – with a dummy front radiator, and on 22nd June 1939 it was transferred, like them, to Grays garage.

Three months later, on 30th September 1939, Q 188 was taken out of service along with various other non-standard vehicles and was destined to spend the first part of the war in storage. At an unknown date it was reactivated as a staff bus for London Aircraft Production, ferrying members of the LAP workforce from Chiswick to Aldenham and Leavesden early each morning and returning them back in the evening. The vehicle did not need to be taxed for this purpose as the use of trade plates for staff transport was then legal, and as a result the exact beginning and ending dates of this operation have not been recorded.

Its end came quite early in the post-war era. At a meeting on 28th February 1946, which also dealt with the fate of the war-damaged Q 217, all the known operational shortcomings of Q 188 were again recited together with the added drawback that for operational purposes it was restricted to certain approved routes. With no department willing to run it, the sale of Q 188 was inevitable.

Like the other three remaining Q double deckers Q 188 was sold to Lancashire Motor Traders, its official date of sale being 28th March 1946. LMT had no trouble finding a buyer for it, and along with the former Q 5 it became a regular feature on H Brown's busy run between Garelochhead and Helensburgh serving the large Faslane naval base on the way. After about five years in scenic Argyllshire it was traded back in to LMT to begin a new stage in its career. From about April 1951 it ran as a furniture transporter for a company in Timperley, Cheshire, now carrying a pantechnicon body and with an extension at the rear bringing it to an overall length of about 30ft. Engine trouble ended its career and resulted in it being scrapped in 1953.

In stark contrast to its former Green Line colours, Q 188 carried an attractive red and cream livery when operating for H Brown & Sons, in whose ownership it is seen outside their substantial garage in Station Road, Garelochhead. *Omnibus Society*

APPENDIX: ROUTES OPERATED IN DETAIL

This appendix was compiled by Malcolm Papes with help from research carried out by Dennis Cox and Ken Glazier. The information was originally published by the London Historical Research Group of the Omnibus Society.

The Q Class in the Central Area

There are two problems concerning the entry into service of the Central Area 5Q5s. Ken Glazier's London Bus File book gives the date each vehicle was taken into stock which is not the same as when it entered service. Similarly, the Schedule Books only indicate the official allocation of number and type to route on a particular date. The date of an entry in the Allocation Book does not necessarily mean that the working started on that day. On the other hand, the day to day variations in rolling stock used in conjunction with the schedules provide a more accurate record of what actually occurred. The date that a bus was licensed to a garage does not necessarily indicate that it commenced working that route on that day.

However, LT had always been economical about a bus only being licensed when actually needed for service. Witness how quickly a bus was delicensed whenever it had a major accident or breakdown, and would not be available for use for some time.

On 4th March 1936, four buses were licensed, Q110/5 at Merton (AL), and Q108/12 at Dalston(D). The AL buses were enough for the two bus requirement on route 200 (Wimbledon Stn-Raynes Park). D however went on receiving the new buses: Q111 on 5th March, Q106/7/17 on 6th March, Q131 on 12th March, Q122 on 12th, Q114/8 on 14th, Q138 on 18th, Q124 on 25th and finally Q132 on 27th March. In total, 13 5Q5s, for route 208 (Bromley-by-Bow-Clapton) which required ten Monday to Friday, 12 on Saturday and 13 on Sunday.

The third garage came into play on 28th March when Q119/23/7/30 were licensed at Chalk Farm (CF). Three more, Q134/7/48, arrived on 3rd April. Then followed Q129 on 9th April, and Q113/45 on 13th. Ten buses were the right number for route 231 (Hampstead Heath-Harlesden). Q141 joined them on 9th May providing a spare for the tight allocation.

AL was the first garage to get a second helping: Q139 on 24th April, Q120 on 30th and Q147 on first of May. Two were for local route 225 (Raynes Park-Grand Drive) which was converted from DA. Q109/57 came to AL on 26th May ready for an extension of 200 to Copse Hill the next day, which doubled its requirement to four Qs.

A fourth garage joined the users of the red 5Q5 when, on 1st May, Q116 was allocated to Old Kent Road (P). Further buses trickled in as follows: Q144 on 4th May, Q121 on 5th, Q126/8 on 7th, Q133/5 on 14th, Q125 on 16th, Q143 on 19th and finally Q150 on 26th May. These replaced the ex-independent single-deckers on the 202 (Rotherhithe-New Cross) with a weekday requirement of nine.

On 25th May, Q136/40/2 were allocated to Kingston (K). These were intended for new weekday route 255 (Feltham-Teddington) which commenced on 27th May. However, on that day they were sent to Harrow Weald (HD) and swapped for three elderly S-types, S386, 425/47 which commenced the new route. The reason for this last minute swap is not known. On 3rd June, however, Q154 was allocated to K, followed by Q158 on 4th and Q149/56 on 8th. This provided the three buses for 255, and the spare was allocated to route 213 (Belmont-Kingston) on weekdays alongside 3 LTLs. On Sundays, all four Qs were used on the 201 (Kingston-Hampton Court extended to Feltham on Sundays).

On 26th May, Q158 had been allocated to HD. As well as the three refugees from K the next day, HD received Q146 on 10th, Q160/5 on 11th and Q161 on 16th. These were used to replace S-types on 230 (North Harrow-Northwick Park) and seven Qs were needed.

It is always said that the last S single-deckers operated from HD on the 230. Indeed, on 17th June 1936, S377,512/3, 890/2 were withdrawn at HD, but on that self-same day, S 386,425/47 were delicensed at K, so who is to say whether it was HD on the 230, or K on the 255 that held the honour of the last operation?

Of the eighty 5Q5s designed for the Central Area, 53 were painted red, and so licensed, but the remaining 27 (Q151/2/5/9,162-4/6-85) were all painted green and sent to the Country Area where they released 4Q4s for Green Line services.

The 5Q5s were not, of course, the first Qs to operate in the Central Area. Q1 had entered service as long ago as 5th September 1932 (LGOC days) on route 11E (Shepherd's Bush-Liverpool Street) from Hammersmith (R). After an experimental period on this busy route, it was transferred to Nunhead (AH) on 28th October 1932 for the 621 (Peckham/Nunhead Circular). It was transferred to the Country Department on 13th February 1934 having just lasted into LPTB days.

A short-lived adventure occurred later in the year when seven 4Q4s were painted red and transferred to the Central Area. On 27th November, Q103 moved into Cricklewood (W). The next day Q101/2/4 arrived, and on 4th December they were followed by Q105. On 9th December T 3,5,10,37 and 50 moved from W to Homchurch (RD), leaving the Qs to take over the five duties on route 226 (Golders Green-Cricklewood Broadway). Also in December Q186/7 were painted red and moved into K, where they worked route 213, alongside the 5Q5 already there, leaving just one LTL.

The 5Q5s were 37-seaters with bodies built by Park Royal, and a front entrance adjacent to the driver. The 4Q4s were also 37-seaters, but were built by the Birmingham Railway and Wagon Company and had a forward entrance, i.e. the entrance was behind the front wheels. 5Q5s were Q106-85 with registrations CLE 129-208. Q101-5 carried plates CGJ206-10, and Q186/7, CLE127/8. The full batch of 4Q4s, Q6-105 were registered BXD 527-576 and CGJ161-210 together with Q186/7.

The stay of 4Q4s was very brief. On 17th February 1937, five Ts were transferred in to W for 226, and Q101-5 went back to the Country Department. Q186/7 left K at the same time, and were replaced by LTLs. The seven buses were part of a batch of 27 which were converted to Green Line Coaches.

Route 255 was withdrawn (LDO 5/10/1937), and 201 was extended to Feltham as on Sunday. It took over the three Qs from the 255, the balance being five LTLs.

On 1st June 1938, route 233 (Finsbury Park-Muswell Hill) was extended via Alexandra Park to Wood Green. At the same time, it was converted from six Ts to 12 Qs, the buses coming from D, and the 208 converting to LTLs. Q106/7/11/2/4/7/8/22/4/9/30/4/8 moved from D to West Green (WG), whilst spare Q158 moved to WG from K. Q138 moved across from WG to HD on 3rd August when 230 was extended from North Harrow to Rayners Lane and required one more bus.

On 12th October 1938, the 231 was extended to Kew Green. This required an additional six Qs on top of the ten which CF was already providing. Another garage came onto he scene when Willesden (AC) was allocated Q116/49/54 from K, and Q181/3-5 from the Country Area, which were painted, red. Route 201 was now entirely operated by eight LTLs, and effectively K ceased to operate the class. This however was to prove short-lived because when on 1st February 1939, route 225 was withdrawn and replaced by double-deck route 50, Q110/5 were transferred from AL to K where they worked together with six LTLs on the 201.

The AC allocation on the 231 was not entirely satisfactory, and from 7th June 1939, Q116/49 /54/81/3-5 were transferred to W to continue with the operation. On 1st November, amid all the reorganisation at the start of the War, the 231 was double-decked and renumbered 70. Q108/13/9/23/7/31/7/41/5 were transferred from CF to K, and Q109/16/43/50/4 also went to K from W. Route 201 could now entirely be converted from LTL to Q, and in addition, route 214 (Kingston-Weybridge) acquired a full allocation of seven Qs replacing the LTLs.

During this chaotic period, it was necessary to introduce a special railway replacement service between Edgware Station and Finchley Station. LOTS record this as commencing on 10th September, the Traffic Circular plumps for Monday 11th September, and the official route card gives 13th December. Operation was from W using five Qs. The rolling stock records are not very helpful in resolving this except that on 16th September Q109/57 are shown as moving from AL to W and Q143/50 from P to W.

During the last four months of 1939 there were reductions in frequencies some of which were found to be too severe, and were adjusted again. Single-deck operation would be wasteful of manpower except that routes involved had some impediment – usually low bridges – to prevent their double-decking. There were movements of 5Q5s to reflect these changes. On 14th November, for example, 233 appears to have had some reductions with Q106/18 moving WG to P, and Q124 WG to AL Two K Qs moved to AL. On 6th December, K lost four Qs, Q148 to P, Q143/5 to WG and Q115 to AL.

The schedules for 13th December 1939 summarise the net result of these movements:

Special Railway Service – W 6/4/4,200 AL 4/4/4,201 K 6/6/8 (with two LTL Saturday & one on Sunday), 202 P 10/10/9, 214 K 5/7/5, 230 HD 8/8/6, and 233 WG 11/10/6. One additional route was involved when P provided one Q for 243 on Saturdays alongside its usual LTLs. This was the Peckham and Nunhead Circular which had operated Q1 on 621 in LGOC days. The 5Q5s were kept well occupied with a maximum of 50 scheduled together with spares.

3rd January 1940 saw one or two adjustments with the 202 increasing to eight Qs, the Special Railway Service reducing from six to five, whilst at HD, the Saturday requirement went up from eight to nine.

Route 241 (Green Street Green/Sidcup Garage and Welling) became very busy as a result of the factories it served, so that on 6th March 1940, it was converted from T to the larger capacity 5Q5s. Q108/10/3/9/23/7/31/7/41 were transferred from

K to Sidcup (SP), and Q149 came from W. The six Ts were replaced by ten Qs. Holloway (J) received the Ts which it placed on route 239 (Tufnell Park-Kings Cross), and its LTLs moved to K. Route 201 was converted from Q to T, and the 214 now had a mixed Q/LTL allocation. The LTLs worked routes 215 and 219/A whilst the Ts which had been used moved across to the 201.

The other change of note for 1940 occurred on 20th November when route 226 was converted to 5Q5. It will be recalled that for a short while in 1937, five Country 4Q4s had been used. Four buses from W were now required, although the actual conversion was complicated by the use of several provincial single-decker loans being used on the route for a few weeks. On the date of conversion, W had allocated Q116/45/8/50/81/83-5, the requirement with the Special Railway Replacement service being nine.

The end result of these changes was that K effectively lost its 5Q5 operation with the 214 fully worked by LTLs on Monday to Friday. In fact, the odd Q did remain at K for quite some months, with Q157 departing on 24 August 1941, and the very last, Q149 two days later, both to SP.

On Wednesday 14th May, the weekday peak requirement on 241 between Sidcup Garage and Welling increased from six to ten bph. The Mon-Fri requirement increased from ten to fourteen Qs, and Saturday to fifteen Qs. One Monday to Friday Q was cross-worked onto the 228 which otherwise saw LTL operation. Q115/20/4/32/9 were transferred to SP from AL on that day. Four Ts moved from SP to K, whilst LT 1040/75/97,1142 went from K to AL to work route 200.

16th May is recorded as the last day of operation of the Special Railway Service, whilst on Saturday 17th May, a new section of 240 was introduced between Edgware and Mill Hill East using LTLs from Edgware (EW). However it was not until 21st May that Q108/54/6/84/5 were transferred from W to AL to convert the 200 back to Qs, and AL's LTLs moved to EW. It is not clear whether the new leg of the 240 was operated at a reduced frequency, or indeed whether the Railway Service operated a few extra days to cover this curious gap.

On 29th October, 241 was withdrawn between Sidcup Garage and Green Street Green, although the frequency over the core section had further increased in the peaks to 12 bph. The allocation now became 11/11/4 Q. Three of the spare Qs were moved to route 228 (Eltham & Chislehurst), so that allocation became: Mon-Fri 3Q,7LTL, Sat 3Q, 5LTL, and Sunday 5Q all from SP. A frequency increase on the 230 at the same time was covered by Q127/37 moving from SP to HD.

The weekday Qs on the 228 were short-lived, and as early as 17th December Q119/23 were swapped with two LTLs from D. On 11th February 1942, the weekday allocation on 241 increased to thirteen Qs when peak hour journeys were introduced between Sidcup Garage and Blackfen. 228 now only saw Qs on Sundays.

On 13th January, Q168 moved into SP from Reigate (RG), and Q174 from Guildford (GF). These were two 5Q5s from the Country Area which were repainted from green to red livery. More were to follow.

Once more Dalston Garage (D) came into the picture. Q119/23 had moved in the previous December, and on 14th January 1942, Q131 also arrived from SP. Q157 went from the same source on 1st March. Seven of the erstwhile green 5Q5s now painted red arrived, all from St Albans (SA) where they were replaced by 4Q4s across the Country Area fleet: 9/3/42 Q172, 10/3/42 Q162/75, 11/3/42 Q151 12/3/42 Q170, and 14/3/42 Q159/67. The LTLs they replaced were put in store. The complete weekday allocation of 6 buses had now changed from LTLs to Qs on the 208A (Clapton-Stratford), and the 208 (Clapton-Bromley-by-Bow) was partly converted: Mon-Fri 3Q,7LTL, Sat 4Q,7LTL and Sun 10Q, 2LTL. Despite the break with traditional design and specifically the positioning of the engine to the offside behind the front axle, the single-decker Qs were reliable, even in the difficult times of the war with its problems of maintenance and spares. The 5Q5s provided maximum space for passengers with their seating capacity for 37 passengers. To increase capacity further, in December 1941 the seating of Q137 was rearranged to perimeter style for 33 passengers, and space was made available for a further 20 standees. The bus was allocated to SP for the busy 241, and during the first ten months of 1942, a substantial proportion of the Central Area Qs were revised in a similar fashion, most reverting back to their former seating between November 1945 and August 1946.

Despite other publications quoting the date of the partial conversion of route 230 to lowbridge double-decker as 28th October 1942, it actually occurred much later using STL19s, Chiswick built lowbridge bodies fitted onto standard STL chassis. STL1955 was allocated to HD on 4th December followed by STL1978 on 17th. The process was speeded up when, on 23rd December, STLs 1617, 1954/73/4,2107 which had been allocated to AL for route 127 were swapped for Q120/7/38/46/61. The 127 (Morden Stn-South Wimbledon Stn) was now temporarily operated with a mixture of Qs and lowbridge STs. STL1979 was allocated to HD on 1st January 1943, and STLs

1990, 2186, 2232 followed. These last three were in brown livery. STL2232 arrived on 1st March, the same day that the last Q, Q132, was transferred out. Interestingly, the 230 retained its number in the single-deck 200s series.

On 28th January 1943, STL2220 was allocated to AL, and they emerged from Chiswick in order STL2217,2292,2250 and finally 2273 on 29th April, STLs 2220 and 2217 in brown. The fifth Q, Q127 left AL on 21st April, and thus ended their short-lived operation on the 127.

The majority of the displaced Qs from both HD and AL were allocated to P which then transferred one of their own vehicles to D, a total of eight for the completion of the conversion of the 208 to the type. The balance went to SP for yet further increases on the 241.

On 1st February Q175, one of the original green examples moved from D to RG where it returned both to Country Area service and livery. Later in April, Q177 also at RG which had never been in red livery was painted grey.

There now followed a period of stability as far as the 5Q5s were concerned. As at 21st April 1943 the disposition of the fleet was as follows:- 200 AL 4/4/3, 202 P 8/8/5, 208 D 10/11/12, 208A D 7/6/0, 226 W 5/4/3, 228 SP 0/0/5. 233 WG 10/10/6. 241 SP 16/16/4. 243 P 0/0/4 (By the October schedule, the Sunday working on the 243 had returned to LTLs).

With a Monday to Friday requirement of 60 Qs, the class was worked hard and any spares or increases had to be covered by vehicles from the LTL or T classes. The one exception was the busy 241 which continued to increase its requirement, and for which extra Qs could be found.

By the end of 1943 service increases on certain of the routes had to be covered by other types. On 1st December, the 200 required a weekday allocation of 6 buses which initially was covered by adding two T's although by April the following year, two extra Qs had been found. On 29th December 241 required three extra weekday buses covered by an extra Q and two Ts. By 19th April 1944 the weekday requirement was 17 Qs and three Ts.

208/A went through a whole series of changes over the next few years. In December 1943, the 208 was rearranged to be worked 6/9/11 Qs and 5/5/0 LTLs. 208A added two weekday Ts to its Q allocation. By 25th October 1944, the allocation on 208 had become 5/9/12 Qs, 2/0/0 Ts, and 4/5/0 LTLs, with the 208A returning to an all Q allocation of 10/6/0. The number of Qs on 208 continued to decline with the balance covered by LTLs. By 7th August 1946, 208 was 2/9/14

Qs, 10/7/0 LTLs, and the 208A required 12/6/0 Qs. On 9th October 1946 there was a swap with 208A converted to LTLs, and 208 becoming 12/14/14 Qs and 0/3/0 LTLs.

On 10th October 1945 Q149/60 were transferred from W to HD for the 230 which needed two more buses. No low-height double-deckers were available so two Qs returned. At W, two LTLs were temporarily allocated for 226. On 21st November STL2217/32 were transferred across from AL where new lowbridge Daimlers were being delivered for the 127. Q149 left HD for SP on 5th December whilst Q160 waited until the first day of the new year before moving to D. Thus ended another short-lived episode.

The increases on SP's busy 241 have been mentioned before. On 12th September 1945 the weekday requirement had increased to 23 buses being made up of seventeen Qs and six Ts. On 13th February 1946 Q146/61 moved from SP to WG for the 233 which now needed twelve Qs. The 241 allocation now became fifteen Qs and eight Ts on weekdays. On 13th June 1946 a further increase changed the allocation to 15/15/8 Qs and 10/10/0 Ts.

On 23rd December 1946, Q142/7 were transferred to WG where the 233 schedule needed 14/14/11 Qs. 241's schedule was now 10/10/10 Qs and 15/14/0 Ts.

In 1946 the pressure on the Central Area single-deck fleet was somewhat relieved by the delivery of 14T12s, post-war members of the T class. Buses of this class which initially were allocated to Muswell Hill (MH) were being replaced by new Leyland TDs, so that 14T12s were reallocated to SP.

The schedules for 30th April 1947 were as follows: 200 AL 6/6/3. 202 P 7/7/4. 208 D 12/14/14 (with three Saturday LTLs), 226 W 5/5/4, 233 WG 14/11/11, and 241 SP 10/10/10 together with 14/14/0 Ts. After eleven years of hectic service, the requirement for 5Q5s had reduced to a maximum of 54, allowing for much needed mechanical attention and an increase in spares.

In the summer of 1948, the Country Area found itself in a position to release the remaining 15 5Q5s to the Central Department. The buses concerned were Q152/66/73/5/7 which were painted red and allocated to SP on 15th July, followed by Q176/8 on 17th and Q164 on 21st. In August Q155 was so treated on 6th, and Q179 on 19th. On 3rd August, Q169/71/80/2 were allocated to W still in green livery for Olympic Games duties. These were then allocated to SP when their special duties ceased, and three worked in the green until repainted at the end of September. Straggler Q163 was not painted green at SP until April 1949. Q175 had been painted red in March 1942, only to return to green in February 1944 before returning to red once more. They had all been released from Reigate (RG) route 447, and Dorking (DS)/Guildford (GF) where they had worked 412 and 425.

The increased requirement at SP was for route 228 whose LTLs were replaced (SP Q11/11/7). By the 13th April 1949 schedules, however, there was an internal reorganisation with the Qs being concentrated on the 241 and the Ts including 14T12s which had worked with the Qs on the 241 going onto the 228. The 241 was the route using the largest number of Qs (SP Q 25/23/12). One interesting effect of this was that on Saturdays SP lent Sutton (A) the two spare Qs for their duties on route 213 for the additional requirement on the service over and above the normal LTL allocation.

In addition, it had been planned that 12 4Q4s be transferred from the Country Area in 1948. In the event, only seven arrived beginning with Q8, 53, 67 which had been painted red and allocated to WG for the 233 on 11th August. Q44 and 68 followed later in the month. On 29th September, Q65 and the last, Q85, entered service on 20th October. Both of these, however, went to D where they worked on the 208A alongside its LTLs. Q85 was classified 1/4Q4/1 since its modification for Green Line duties in 1937, although it had reverted back to Country Bus duties in 1938. All the others were plain 4Q4s. The five 4Q4s with their forward rather than front doors which had to be roped open to comply with the strict Metropolitan Police regulations for Central buses were not found to be suitable on the 233, so from 15th November they were swapped with 5Q5s from D, and then worked on the 208. Their stay at D was hardly less happy and early in 1949 they returned to the Country Area, the last to leave D being Q68 on 15th March. Q67 and 68 were painted back into green, but the other five retained their red livery. 208A once again was worked entirely by LTLs, whilst the 208 used 5Q5s with LTL support especially at weekends.

1949 was a quiet year for Qs in the Central Area. On 26th October, 233 was extended to Northumberland Park Station and needed an extra 3 buses. At first two Ts from HD made up the shortfall, but on 14th December, the busy 226 was converted to double-deck so releasing a handful of Qs. On the same day, 233 had an increase in frequency needing three more Qs so that Q118/45/51/67 moved from W to WG. The 241 had an increase in its Mon-Fri peak frequency needing another two Qs in the form of Q113/27 from W to SP. During this period of vehicle shortages, W had been in the habit of using any spare bus including the odd Q for peak hour duties on its busy double-deck route 16 (Sudbury Town-Victoria Stn), but this practice now had to cease.

1950 began with a flurry when on 23rd January 4Q4s 35 and 59 moved into K as trainers. The garage's allocation was almost entirely single-deck with its routes mainly going out into the Surrey suburbs and villages. Despite an allocation of TDs, there was a substantial proportion of LTLs and Ts (including ex-Green Line 1/7T7/1s) being withdrawn whilst others were being fitted with oil engines from scrapped STLs. On 6th February, Q44 and Q65 entered service at K with Q8 on 4th March. On 26th March, Q10/3/5/6,53,85 joined them. Q6 and Q20 followed on 26th April, Q2 1 ,67 on 1st May and finally Q26 on 9th June.

Q8, 44, 53, 65 and 85 were still in red livery from their previous operation in the Central Area whilst Q6, 16,20/1/6 were painted red during the year. The others remained green throughout their stay at Kingston. In addition to these Qs which were allocated to K, Q9,11/2, 23/8, 38, 45, 69, 71/3,99 and 101, all in green livery, were loaned on an ad hoc basis throughout the summer especially at weekends to cover for increased frequencies, from Reigate (RG). Incidentally, the two trainers, Q35 and 59 were returned to the Country Area as early as February 1950. The 4Q4s were mainly allocated to routes 215 (Kingston-Ripley) and 219 (Kingston -Weybridge). By the end of the summer, fourteen Qs were required on the joint Monday-Friday allocation. On Sundays, the 218 (Kingston-Staines) was included, although Qs were not allowed to work over Walton Bridge. In 1951, the three routes had a joint daily allocation (K Q14/13/16 and K T 19/17/19). Photographic evidence indicates that 4Q4s were often to be found on the 213 alongside the scheduled Ts, whilst A borrowed 5Q5s from SP to supplement the LTLs at weekends.

It was the 1/4Q4/1 Q85 which was the first to be withdrawn on 20th May 1952. In June 1952, Q18 came to K, joined by Q42 and 64 in September. On 14th May, Norbiton (NB) opened to relieve the pressure at K, and the 213 was one of the routes allocated there, which meant that 4Q4s no longer officially appeared on that service. However, an Alan Cross photo of Q178 dated 7th June 1952 is clearly coded. NB 15 showing that loans must have taken place. 4Q4s gradually disappeared from K, with Q6,8,26 being withdrawn on 20th November, and the last pair, Q42 and 64 being withdrawn on 25th March 1953, which was the last day of any Q1 operation in the Central Area. Replacements were mainly in the form of TDls, which were released at Muswell Hill (MH) when new RFs were introduced there as well as later models released from Southall (HW) where 14Tl2s from SP took over on route 211.

Incidentally, another green 4Q4, Q69 was often loaned to SP from Northfleet (NF) during this same period.

The schedule for 17th October 1951 forms a useful summary before the relative stability of the class was broken: 200 AL Q 6/6/5. 202 P Q 7/7/5. 208 D Q 13/14/16, LTL 0/4/3. 213 A Q 0/2/0, LTL 21/20/18 (plus K), 215/8/9 Q 14/13/16, T 19/17/19. 233 WG Q 22/21/19, 241 SP Q 27/22/12. The total requirement was 75 5Q5s and 14 4Q4s.

On 31st March 1951, an urgent need for driver training buses arose. Q153 (WG) and Q125 (AL) were withdrawn for training purposes at their own garages, and Q141 (D), Q120 (P), and Q136 (SP) were sent to Riverside (R), Camberwell (Q) and Streatham (AK) respectively. These were temporarily replaced by green 10T10s T465 (D), T473 (P), T485 (WG) and T525 (AL). The requirement was short-lived, and by 3rd May the Qs had returned to service and the Ts went back to their Country garages.

There was one final surprise for Q operation in the Capital. The prestige Green Line services were upgraded with new RFs which meant that the Central single-deck fleet had to wait until this process had taken place. Even the renovated LTLs were showing their age, no more so than at MH where together with the TDs, they worked some of the busiest single-deck routes. On 1st March 1952, a number of 6Q6s descended on MH for training purposes Q194/8, 206/21/32/5/8.

The batch Q189-238 (CXX382-406, DGX220-244) were longer wheel-base forward entrance buses with Park Royal bodies which had worked as Green Line coaches, apart from during the War when they had been converted to ambulances. They had mainly just been withdrawn, although one or two had found work supporting the Country Area bus fleet. They were now being pressed into stop-gap service allowing LTLs to be withdrawn before new Central Area red RFs could be delivered.

On 19th March 1952, Q191/4/8/11/200/3/4/8/11/ 2*/5/6*/8*/21/2*/4/30/2/3/5/7*/8 entered service at MH replacing eighteen LTLs. On 1st May, Q194/8, 206/8/ 16*/21 were taken out of service for training, staff bus duties etc, and Q192, 213*/25 and 229 took their place. They were all in Green Line livery and were not modified other than to have the Green Line name replaced by London Transport, and the doors roped open. Vehicles marked * had not come directly from the Green Line fleet, but had been used as buses prior to their allocation to MH.

These were used on routes 210 (Finsbury Park-Golders Green) and 244 (Muswell Hill-Winchmore Hill). At the schedule for 14th May 1952, the allocation was shown as 210 MH Q 8/4/12, TD 6/13/11 and 244 MH Q 6/9/8.

On 10th September, brand new RFs 289/91/3 were allocated to MH and Q191/2,224 were withdrawn. The process of replacement continued until 11th December when the last two 6Q6s, Q230/8 were withdrawn. Basically, the 210 received the new RFs, allowing the TDs to move over to the 244, and the 6Q6s to be withdrawn, but it took some three months to achieve with the odd hiccup.

The 5Q5s had given sixteen years of reliable service on some of the busiest routes, all the more remarkable because of their unconventional design, and that they operated throughout the War with the minimum of attention. Odd examples started to be withdrawn in 1952 – the very first being Q130 at P on 16th April. Q152 followed on 20th May and Q182 on 17th June, both also from P. July 1st saw the withdrawal of Q106 (AL), and on 15th July Q108 (AL) followed. On 21st October Q129 (D) saw its last service.

Red RFs began to flood in and the usual process began with the bulk of the 5Q5s from each conversion being withdrawn, but odd examples being transferred to cover shortages due to early withdrawals at other garages.

On 11th and 12th December route 200 at AL was converted to RF. Q125/6/54/7 went to SP, whilst Q109 went to D, and Q160 to WG. The transfer of serviceable Qs to SP allowed its 14T12s to move to HW, whose TDs on route 211 then went to K for replacement of its ageing fleet including the 4Q4s. At SP, this meant a temporary part allocation of Qs on the 228 which, of course, was no stranger to the class.

In December, new RFs moved into P for the conversion of route 202, and a few more Qs were available for SP to release 14T12s. It should be remembered that new RFs were not just replacing Qs, but also other time-worn classes at other garages.

The first major loss of 5Q5s in 1953 occurred at WG on 1st February with a requirement of 22 RFs plus spares to replace the Qs on the 233. Most of the displaced buses were withdrawn, with Q132/7 moving to SP, and Q136/47/84 to D.

D itself lost its Qs in February when they were replaced on the 208 by RFs. 208A with its allocation of LTLs had seen these replaced by RFs a few months earlier.

This left SP with the largest single allocation of 5Q5s. From 1st March, RFs started to replace Qs on both the 241 and the short-lived allocation on the 228 rapidly. They were all now withdrawn when taken out of service.

The final day of Q operation on Central Area routes occurred on 25th March.

The Country Area Buses and Coaches

The Q class vehicles in the Country Area were just as ultra-modem as their red cousins in the Central Area. Of course, Q1 had been painted green and transferred to Reigate (RG) on 13th February 1934. It was so successful that an order for 102 4Q4s was made and these formed the backbone of the green single-deck bus fleet for many years. Unlike the 5Q5s, these were of a forward entrance layout with the door behind the front wheels. They were delivered as 37-seaters with a double seat beside the driver, but between March and September 1936, this was removed reducing the seating to 35, and a full-width bulkhead with a centrally placed communicating door was fitted. Q186/7, which were delivered later, had this feature as new. They were all bodied by the Birmingham Railway and Wagon Company.

The Traffic Circulars were peppered with references to complaints from passengers that conductors were using the communicating door to talk to the driver when the vehicle was in motion. The instructions were that the door should be firmly closed except in hot weather, when it should be opened to allow ventilation.

Unlike the 5Q5s, where passenger doors were forbidden by the Metropolitan Police in the Central Area, the crews were instructed that the doors should be closed at all times, other than when the bus was passing through towns and villages!

The registrations came very near to being in sequence, a novel feature for London buses at this time. Q6-55 were registered BXD 527-39/41/0/2-76, and Q56-105 were CGJ 161-93/5/4/6-210. Q186/7 were CLE 127/8.

The first 4Q4 to enter service was Q8 on 6th July 1935 at Watford High Street (WA). There were to be sixteen in all. Throughout July they commenced service as follows: Q10 (10th), Q9 (11th), Q7 (12th), Q11 (16th), Q6, 13/6 (21st) Q19 (29th), and Q22 (30th). Licensing continued in August: QI7 (1st), and Q25-7 (3rd), but then there was a slight gap until October with the arrival of Q52 (12th) and Q81 (29th). This was the largest allocation to one garage, and they were to be found on route 306 (Watford-Enfield via Bushey Heath), 312 (Watford-Enfield via Little Bushey), 311/A (Watford-Borehamwood/Radlett) and 335 (Watford-Windsor).

The route detail given is sufficient only to identify where it ran. There were many short workings and intermediate variations which are not shown here. In the Country Area there was also a great deal of interworking and mixed allocations so that the pattern is far more complicated than for the 5Q5s in the Central Area.

The second garage to get an allocation was Dartford (DT) in the Southern Area. Q12 entered service on 16th July, was followed by Q14/5 (19th), Q18,20/1 (24th) and Q24 (on 1st August). Q18 may not in fact have worked from DT, as it moved to Amersham (MA) within a very few days. The buses were for route 499 (Erith-Famingham).

Amersham (MA) on the north-west edge of the LPTB statutory area received Q23 on 1st August followed by Q28 and Q29 on the 3rd. Q18 was the fourth bus. These were used on the complex 353/362 group of services. 353 (Ley Hill-Windsor), 362 (Ley Hill-High Wycombe) and 362A (Holmer Green-IIigh Wycombc).

Still in the Northem Area, Hertford (HG) received a substantial allocation spread over three months. The deliveries in August were Q30 (3rd), Q32 (16th), Q34 (18th), and Q31/5 (21st). September saw Q33 (4th), Q56 (21st), and then in October, Q70 (3rd), Q69 (5th), Q71 (11th) and Q72 (12th). These were used on routes 303 (New Barnet-Hitchin), 303A (Knebworth-Welwyn Garden City Theatre Bus), 342 (New Barnet-Hertford) and 340/1 (St Albans-Bishops Stortford/Stanstead Abbots). The evening 303A was withdrawn on 14th August 1935 and a new daily service between Hatfield and Welwyn Garden City was introduced on 27th November under the 303A number. The 340 was amended on the same day to operate between St Albans and Hertford via Cole Green, whilst 341 was also altered to terminate at these same points but via Bayford Turn.

The Allocation Book gives an instruction that a fare table should be carried for route 333 also. This was common in the Country Area, and meant that during the course of the day, the bus would work an odd journey on that particular route. On occasion, this would be no more than a garage journey using the roads of another service.

Hatfield (HF) had a minority interest in routes 303/A and 340/1. On 24th August, Q36 and Q37 were allocated, followed by Q86, the very last of the main batch to enter service on 3rd January 1936.

So far, the Northern Area had had the lion's share, but now it was the turn of Leatherhead (LH). Q38/40 went into service on 24th August, Q41/3/4 followed on 2nd September, and straggler Q82 arrived on 29th October. These were used on the 418 (Kingston-Leatherhead/Effingham). In the next summer, they were also to be found on the seasonal 418B linking Epsom with Chessington Zoo.

The other Watford Garage, Leavesden Road (WT), was next to receive a substantial allocation in the early autumn. The September deliveries involved Q39/46-50 (7th), Q60 (27th) and Q61-3/5 (30th).

Q66/7 (3rd) and Q64/8 (4th) followed in October. These buses were used on the 317 and 318 groups as well as the 385 (Watford Met Stn-Radlett Road).

Swanley Junction (SJ) received Q42 on 2nd September and Q51/3-5 twelve days later for its share on the 499. Buses were instructed to carry fare tables for double-deck trunk routes 401, 423 and 477 additionally.

One of the main functions for the 4Q4s was to replace the great variety of vehicle types which had been acquired with the take-over of numerous small operators. Reigate (RG) which had been the first Country garage to operate the Q in the form of Q1, was now about to receive some 4Q4s. Q45 was a forerunner on 2nd September, whilst in October it was joined by Q76 (21st) and Q78-80 (22nd). Q1 had been working route 427 (Reigate and Redhill Circular), with turns on the Saturday only 460 (South Merstham-Meadvale) and 440 (South Merstham-Salfords). The five additions were intended for 429 (Dorking-Newdigate), 439 (Dorking-South Merstham) and 430 (Reigate-South Merstham).

Staying in the south, Dunton Green (DG) received Q58/9 on 21st September for route 454 (Sevenoaks-Tonbridge). Four Qs were allocated to Addlestone (WY) during the autumn: Q57 on 21st September, Q73 on 14th October, and Q102/3 on 30th November. These were needed for 436 (Guildford-Uxbridge). Two buses went to Godstone (GD) with Q74 on 14th October, and Q75 two days later. These were for the 449 (Woldingham-Redhill). A fare table was required for route 410.

Dorking (DS) was next in line with Q83-5 on 29th October, and Q77 on 1st November. These four buses covered four routes, 429 and 439 shared with RG, as well as 425 (Dorking North- Guildford) and 412 (Dorking North-Holmbury St Mary). This last route was of interest in that the bus was out-stationed overnight at Holmbury St Mary.

Guildford (GF) received its eight 4Q4s through November: Q87 (1st), Q88, 90 (5th), Q89 (7th) and Q92-5 (13th). These were for two routes shared with other garages – 436 with WY and WR and 425 with DS. Also the recipient of eight new buses was Windsor (WR). The November deliveries were Q91 (7th), Q96/7 (16th) and Q98-101 (30th). Q105 followed on 13th December. These were also for routes shared with other garages, 335 and 436.

This left just Q104 which was delivered to St Albans (SA) on 13th December. This same garage also took the two late arrivals Q186 on 6th July 1936, and Q187 the next day. Route details will be covered a little later.

Thus, the entire fleet of 4Q4s had been delivered and were in service. This was a time of reorganisation in the Country Area and stability was not to be established.

The first big changes were part of the Watford area reorganisation on 18th March 1936. Effectively, the 4Q4s at WT were replaced by R and T class buses. The Rs were AEC Reliances which had just been rebodied with very attractive Weymann 30-seaters in 1935, and now replaced the Qs on the 317 group, whilst the 318 was withdrawn. WA, already the largest single operator of Qs, now added a further four from WT and one from GF to its total. (Q50, 60-2 ex WT and Q95 ex GF.) There was a considerable revision to its routes at the same time and its small allocations of Rs and Ts (AEC Regals) were transferred away.

Two other garages to benefit were HG which received Q63-6, and HF (Q39, 46-8) all from WT replacing Rs, Ts and GFs (Gilfords) which went elsewhere.

Route 436 was completely reorganised too, with the Windsor Castle-Uxbridge section being covered by a new 458, and the Windsor-Guildford section retaining the number 436. However, the allocation from all three garages saw the Qs replaced by Rs. WR's Qs were replaced by Rl-4 ex WA, and R44 ex HH leaving Qs just for 335, and WY's were replaced by R5, 11-3,29 ex Northfleet (NF). GF also received R6-8 leaving a reduced Q allocation for the 425.

The displaced Qs included an allocation of six (Q57,73,91,102/3 ex WY), and Q105 (ex WR) to Northfleet (NF) for the first time. The Kent garage operated both infrequent country routes as well as works services covering the industrialised estuary. The main recipients were 489 (Ash-Gravesend) and local Gravesend service 497.

Q93/9 ex GF went to RG in a direct swap with R 7, 8 whilst Q98-101 left WR for St Albans (SA), which was starting to build up an allocation of the type.

Starting in August, twenty-seven of the Central Area order for eighty 5Q5s were delivered in green livery for the Country Area. These carried Park Royal bodies with a front entrance, and, of course, as they were intended for the Central Area, had no doors. Nevertheless they were the sleekest and most attractive of all the Q bodies. Four Country Area garages were selected for their initial allocation:-

HG: Q171/4/6/9 (1st Aug.), Q170 (19th Aug.) and Q177, 182 (1st Sept.)

HF: Q159/62/4/6/70/8/9 (1st Aug.), Q173 (13th Aug.), Q175 (21st Aug.)

NF: Q151/5/63/8/72/80 (1st Aug.)

MA: Q183 (1st Sept.), Q181 (2nd Sept.), Q184/5 (3rd Sept.) and Q152 (7th Sept.).

Displaced 4Q4s from HG moved to SA Q55,64/5/9 and WA (Q30/3/5).

Displaced 4Q4s from HF moved to WT (Q37/9, 47/8) and Staines (ST) (Q36,46,86).

There were two displacements from MA being Q18, 29 which moved to High Wycombe (HE).

NF transferred Q57, 91 to LH on 15th August, but otherwise kept 4Q4s until 1st October where they worked as extras including duplicates on Green Line A1 and A2 (Gravesend-Ascot/Sunningdale). It seems likely that the three 4Q4s transferred to ST would also have worked as duplicates on Green Line A1, A2 and also D (Staines-Sevenoaks).

The return of 4Q4s to WT is noteworthy, the four buses replacing three Ts and an R.

The build-up of 4Q4s at SA had been a slow process and were now to be found on the 338 (St Albans-London Colney), 343 (St Albans-Enfield), 354 (St Albans/Fleetville Circular), 355 (Radlett Stn-Harpenden) and. 358 (St Albans-Shenley).

SA lost Q101/4 to Luton (LS) on 24th September. These replaced T38,396 at LS which went to Romford (London Road) (RE), and to complete the triangle GF94,102 moved to SA. It would seem the Gilfords worked route 343.

During this busy period, DG left the ranks of Q operators when its two-bus allocation on 454 was replaced by T372/3. Q58 was transferred to MA and Q59 to SJ on 3rd September.

Another upheaval took place on 1st October 1936. Twenty-three 4Q4s were delicensed. Two more followed on 27th, and on 31st Q81/3 were also taken out of service. They were all within the batch Q81-105/86/7 and the twenty-seven coincided with a similar number of 5Q5s introduced to the Country Area. The withdrawals had been delayed until the end of the summer augmentation period. There were a considerable number of transfers to fill the gaps, although the 5Q5s remained together in their batches. Of note was the loss of the temporary allocation of 4Q4s at ST and LS.

A decision had been taken to convert the twenty-seven 4Q4s to Green Line duties with the addition of heaters, interior luggage racks and brackets for side indicator boards. A radiator was fitted at the front and the Green Line fleet name was added. They were then reclassified 1/4Q4/1s. The 1936 renewal programme had already included one hundred new coaches – fifty Qs classified 6Q6 (Q189-238) and fifty AEC Regals, the 9T9s. However, this order would not cover the replacement of the remaining GF Gilfords on Green Line duty and hence the plan to use some 4Q4s. Over the coming months the conversion programme proceeded.

All of the single-deck Qs proved themselves reliable and solid workhorses. However it is notable that, after the 6Q6s, orders returned to conventional layout buses. There were problems with the Traffic Commissioners in certain areas getting the buses licensed to particular routes, and this was exacerbated by their insistence on treating 4Q4s and 5Q5s as different types.

Also on 1st October, Q152/81-3/5 were transferred from MA to HE thereby releasing HE's 4Q4s and some Ts to other garages. MA also lost Q23/8,58 at the same time. Then on 9th October, NF sent Q151/5/63/8/72/80 to SA in exchange for 4Q4s. In early November, SA also acquired Q171/4/6/9/82 from HG. MA, which had temporarily lost a portion of its Q fleet for Ts, began to build up its 4Q4s once more: Q63-5/71 from SA, and Q34,56 from HG. MA was then able to shed T15,21/5,35,375/84 to HG to complete the triangle. Later in the month, WT was also able to release Q39,67/8 to MA.

A curious occurrence took place when seven of the 4Q4s awaiting conversion were painted red and allocated to the Central Area: Q101-5 to Cricklewood (W) for their route 226, and Q186/7 to Kingston (K). It might have been expected that seven of the 5Q5s be used instead. This took place between 27th November and 4th December, and proved to be short-lived. On 17th February 1937, Q186/7 left K to be allocated to ST for two weeks and on the 1st March Q101-5 were delicensed at W. They were subsequently painted green and converted to 1/4Q4/1s.

1937-1938

A new garage to the operation of the Q was East Grinstead (EG) when, on 31st January 1937, Q70/2 were transferred from NF to replace two Rs on route 424 (Reigate-East Grinstead).

The first of the Green Line conversions entered service on 6th March – Q81/6,95/8 at HG and Q87/8 at RG. Those at HG worked with the 6Q6s allocated there for routes M1/2/3 linking Hertford with Byfleet, Guildford and Esher, whilst the RG examples worked alongside the 9T9s on route J (Watford-Reigate). These trials were satisfactory so from 25th March, 1/4Q4/1s entered normal service as follows:

NF: Q92-4, 100/4/5 together with Q87/8 (A1 /2 Gravesend-Ascot/Sunningdale)

ST: Q96/7,101-3, 186/7. (A1/2 as above)

LH: Q82-5/9-91 (L Uxbridge-Great Bookham)

MA: Q99 together with Q81/6,95/8 (Q High Wycombe-Oxford Circus) ·

The L was withdrawn (LDO 1st May) and its l/4Q4/1s were reallocated: Q82-4 (WT), Q85 (NF), Q89/90 (HE) and Q91 (GF). Those at WT were used on route T (Watford-Golders Green). The balance was available as duplicates working alongside 6Q6s as necessary.

At last there followed a period of stability. One exception occurred on 7th July when HE transferred its 5Q5s, Q152/81/3-5 to WA in exchange for Q30/3/5,60/2.

The first Country Area Allocation of Scheduled Buses and Coaches was issued for the period commencing July 7th 1937, and this provides a good occasion to summarise the operation of the Country Qs after about two years in service.

On 6th October 1937, route 461 which had used Cubs and operated between Walton and Ottershaw was amended. The revised 461 ran between Hersham and Staines with a Saturday pm extension to Slough Station. From 9th February 1938, it was further amended to work between Slough and Walton on Saturdays instead of to Hersham. Returning to October, new route 461A was introduced between Hersham and Ottershaw. Both were worked by WY, 461 being 4Q4 2/2/2, and 461A 4Q4 3/3/3. Fare tables were carried for route 462 in both cases.

The buses transferred to WY were Q7 (ex WA), Q42 (ex DT), Q47/8 ex WT and Q77 ex DS.

The two buses from WT had been used on route 385 which now used Rs. The example from DT was the result of a reduction of its Monday-Friday requirement from 5 to 4 4Q4s on the 499.

A week later, route 343 (St Albans-Welham Green) was converted from DL class Dennis Arrow to 5Q5 (SA 5Q5 2/2/1). At the same time, the single 1/4Q4/1 at GF, Q91 was transferred to WT so that Green Line route T could now be fully operated with the type.

3rd November saw another batch of changes, 5Q5s Q151/5/63/74 were transferred from SA to GF and Q180/2 to DS. This enabled the 425 from both GF and DS to be converted from 4Q4 to 5Q5, whilst DS also used one on the 429 and 439. Q23/8,46,58 moved from GF to SA whilst Q36/7 went in the same direction from DS.

Routes 354 and 355 at SA now used the 4Q4. The Wed/Sat/Sun service 382 (Sandridge-Codicote) was also converted to 5Q5 for which one bus was required. On 10th November, 338 was converted from 5Q5 to ST releasing its one bus for this purpose.

On 3rd November, EG swapped R15 with Q18 so that its route 424 could now be fully worked by three 4Q4s. The single bus on 412 at DS now used the Reliance.

By the issue of Allocation No.3 dated 9th February 1938, route 427 which was host to Q1 now had a daily operation of two 4Q4s in place of Rs from RG. This included a journey on the 440A. A RG Q operating routes 429 and 439 was now required to carry a Fare Table for the 414.

At the same date, route 343 was converted from two 5Q5s to double-decker with STs. The 5Q5s at SA immediately found a fresh home on new route 391A, a local service between a Townsend and Hill End which required six buses, three 5Q5s and three Ts.

The same schedule showed that the 6Q6s for routes Ml, M2 and M3 operating from WR, WY and HG worked journeys on the 456, 462 and 310 before they went onto their Green Line duties. One bus also covered a journey on the C2 (Tunbridge Wells-Woking).

On 6th April, route 499 was shortened to work between Dartford and Farningham. The busier western section was covered by double-deck route 480, which was expanded to run between Erith and Denton. At the same time the allocations at both SJ and DT were converted to T.

Q20/1 moved from DT to GF and Q53/4/9 from SJ to WY to replace Rs on 436 (Staines-Guildford) and 436A (Staines Ripley) with three Qs each from both GF and WY. Q15 moved from DT to HG where it replaced the 5Q5 on route 340. The spare 5Q5 went on to the 331 (Hertford-Buntingford-Hertford) replacing an R daily.

There were several reasons for the apparent instability of the Q class allocations. Throughout this period, the Country Department of LPTB was in the process of withdrawing the older saloons some of which had been taken over from independents. The R class was in the process of withdrawal, and the Weymann bodies from those which had been rebodied were placed on certain T class chassis. Some of the earlier of the T class themselves were in the process of withdrawal too. Green Line 10T10s were starting to flood in and displace older coaches which were relegated to bus work (the 7T7s). This was a period of growth for many towns and villages in the Home Counties and with the increase in demand, saloons with a larger capacity were required. Examples have already been noted of routes being converted from single to double deck. The Qs were moved around to take account of these changing requirements.

Considering the R class was being withdrawn, it was surprising that on 11th May, LH's route 418 was converted from 4Q4 to R. Q12,44 moved to SA which displaced T99, 107 to MA which in turn sent R6,7 to LH. Q38,40 were swapped with R19,20 at EG, Q41 was swapped with R at WT whilst Q43 went to RG and spare R33 came from HG. At WT, route 385 once more converted to 4Q4 with its one bus allocation, whilst at EG the 428 (East Grinstead-Dolmansland) joined the ranks of Q operation (EG Q 1/2/1). At RG, route 406C (Earlswood-Kingswood) swapped a T for the 4Q4. By the new allocation listing at 1st June, the weekend 365 at SA now used a pair of 4Q4s instead of 5Q5s.

On 6th July, there were further upheavals when the 306 was upgraded from 4Q4s to double-decker STs. The 312, which had been jointly scheduled, was separated out and continued to use two 4Q4s from WA daily. 311/A was converted from 5Q5s to 4Q4s using four made redundant from 306.

On 7th July, Q19 went from WA to SA where it replaced a T on the Wed/Sat/Sun route 382 (Sandridge Codicote). Q50 was transferred to HE where it worked the one bus requirement on weekday route 455A (West Wycombe-Wooburn Common). Q26/7 went to Hemel Hempstead (HH) although it is not clear whether they were specifically allocated to a route or whether they were spares. In any case, they only stayed there until 1st October, but it was new territory for the class. 5Q5s Q152/81/3-5 moved to WR in readiness for changes there early in August.

There were also changes south of London on 6th July. Route 430 was converted from 4Q4 to ST at RG. Three new routes were introduced: 447 (Reigate-South Merstham), 447A (Reigate-South Merstham via Main Road), and 447B (Reigate-South Merstham via Blackborough Road). Two RG 4Q4s were needed for the three routes, and the other 4Q4 spare from the 430 was used on the 427 which became two Q, ex one, and one T.

On 1st August, 10T10s replaced the 1/4Q4/1s on Green Line routes A1 and A2 at both ST and NF. The displaced vehicles were reallocated as follows: Q87,96/7, 101-3 ST to SA, Q186/7 ST to WY, Q88,92 NF to CY, Q93/4 NF to EG and Q104/5 NF to DG. At SA, 5Q5s were replaced by the 1/4Q4/1s such that Q168/7/2 were transferred to HG, and Q176/8 went to WR. Over the coming days, after the 1/4Q4/1s had been prepared for bus work, including the removal of the heaters, Green Line names and side boards, they re-entered service. 355 at SA used five 4Q4s instead of a mix of 4Q4s and 5Q5s, and this was also the case with the 391A which became SA 4Q4 6/6/4. The three 5Q5s at HG were enough to convert route 331 fully to the type displacing the remaining Ts (HG 5Q5 3/3/2). On Saturdays 5Q5 was also able to work journeys on 329 (Knebworth-Hertford) and 329A (Hitchin-Datchworth).

Over at WR, route 457 (Windsor-Uxbridge) had already started to use 5Q5s. From 4th August, it was recast with three additional routes 457A (Slough Station-George Green), 457B (Windsor Pinewood Studios), and 457C (Uxbridge Pinewood Studios). The requirement was 457/A WR 5Q5 (3/3/3), and 457B/C WR 4Q4 (2/2/1).

In the Southern Area, route 434 (Horsham-Edenbridge) was converted to 4Q4 from both EG (2/2/2) and Crawley (CY) (2/2/2) in each case replacing Ts. Route 454 (Sevenoaks-Tonbridge) also replaced its Ts and now became Dunton Green (DG) 4Q4 (1/2/2). At NF, the 489 which had used one T and one Q now employed two 4Q4s. The two additional Qs at WY were for route 461 which used four 4Q4s on Saturday in place of two Qs and two Ts. One unrelated event was the replacement of the 4Q4 for a Cub at LH on the Chessington 418B.

On 1st September, the balance of the 1/4Q4/1s were displaced from Green Line duties at WT, HE and MA by new 10T10s for routes T, and Q and R in part. The displaced vehicles were Q81 MA to HE, Q86 MA to TG, Q95 MA to SA, Q82/3 WT to GF, Q91 WT to RG and Q84 WT to NF. This returned twenty-six of the twenty-seven to bus work, some of which remained at their existing garage for conversion and re-entry into service. The missing vehicle Q100 had been delicensed at NF on 14th July, perhaps because of an accident or major breakdown, and when it returned to service remained as a Green Line coach not finally being converted until 1948, although, of course, it worked as a bus through the War when the Green Line network was suspended.

The spare buses were then used to convert routes 305 (Gerrards Cross-High Wycombe) and 455 (High Wycombe-Uxbridge). HE used two 4Q4s daily in place of Rs, and MA's allocation was 4Q4 2/2/1 in place of Ts. Another new garage to the class was Tring (TG) which needed just one Q for 387 (Tring Station-Aldbury). Two 4Q4s at GF replaced the Ts on route 415 (Guildford-Ripley).

On 1st October 1938, Q26/7 ex HH, Q57 ex LH, and Q151 ex DS were transferred to WR and 5Q5s Q181/3-5 were withdrawn, painted red, and sent to the Central Area where they were needed for changes to route 231.

One small change in the schedule published for October 1938 was for the Sunday only route 349 (Watford-Hertford) to use a 4Q4 rather than a T from WA. Then on 1st November 1938, Q151 moved from WR to HG where the latter garage's contribution to 340/1 converted from 4Q4 to 5Q5.

1939-1940

The first part of 1939 was quiet after the upheavals of the previous year. On 3rd January, Q29,45 moved from RG to GF in return for T232/6. Route 427 was thus amended to T operation whilst route 438 (Guildford-Woking) was altered to 4Q4. There was an instruction that one of the buses should carry a fare table for the 408.

On 25th January, TG's solitary Q86 for route 387 was swapped with T217 from WR. Then on 30th January, WR swapped 5Q5s Q152/76/9 for GF's 4Q4s Q73,82/3. Route 457/A was now converted to 4Q4s whilst GF's 415 employed the 5Q5s.

During this period, SA (Q87,95) and CY (Q88 92) swapped these l/4Q4/ls with WT (Q41,57) and RG (Q43/4) 4Q4s respectively. The reason is not recorded although the former Green Line vehicles still had their luggage racks and may have been needed for coach relief duties at busy times.

The last Country Area Allocation of Scheduled Buses and Coaches (No.6) before the War was published for the period commencing 24th May 1939 and forms a useful basis of summarising the hectic changes which had already taken place.

Preparations for war had been taking place ever since the Munich Crisis and for the period leading up to the Declaration of War on 3rd September 1939 there were very few changes.

Then on 1st September the entire Green Line network was suspended and the fleet of coaches including all the 6Q6s were converted to ambulances and attached to Central Area garages.

In the Country Area there was a lot of activity, first helping the Central Area with the Evacuation, and then dealing with movements of both troops and essential workers. There were a number of important factories in the Home Counties perhaps none more so than the Vickers Aircraft factory in Weybridge. Leisure travel especially in the evenings had greatly reduced whereas demand for essential travel during the day increased in many areas.

Substantial numbers of staff had been called up and the diversion of resources including fuel meant that services were adjusted to the prevalent demand. Whereas this had a major impact on buses, routes and frequencies in the Central Area, in the Country Area the need for increased capacity sometimes made the alterations less severe. The reliable 4Q4s and 5Q5s with their oil engines were fully employed.

At the end of September, the Government announced a 25% cut in fuel supplies and from 29th there had to be a major delicensing of buses and substantial cuts in services. The Country Area did not escape. However, as far as the 4Q4s and 5Q5s were concerned, they were immediately redeployed elsewhere: Q42,77 WY to EG, Q47 WY to RG, Q61/,6 WR to SA, Q87,95 WT to HG, Q170 HG to HF and Q31 NF to MA. It is not possible to identify the use to which these vehicles were put at their new garages except to say that local unscheduled duplicates were needed on the busiest routes. Certain large factories chartered buses to ensure transport for their staff. In the Schedules for 13th March 1940, it is recorded that the following were used for private hire over and above the scheduled route requirement: HF two 5Q5s, HG two 5Q5s, SA three 4Q4s, and MA three 4Q4s. Certain Works activity did not appear in the Schedule Books. It is noteworthy amongst the 29th September transfers, Qs were being transferred away from WY with its expected needs of the Vickers factory, but within weeks the movements were in the opposite direction. One especially interesting transfer from HG to WY took place on 18th November when the sole remaining 1/4Q4/l coach, Q100, arrived.

On 22nd November, Q46,58,64 went from SA to WY, on 14th December Q34 from MA to WY and Q87 from HG to WY. Two days later, Q80 went from RG to WY. .

Q53 was transferred from WY to TG on 12th October followed by Q95 from HG to TG on 8th November. Local route 387 was converted back to the class again. One of the earliest war-time route changes took place from 4th October when 454 (Tonbridge-Sevenoaks) was extended to Chipstead via Bat and Ball. On Monday to Friday, there was also an extension via Tubs Hill numbered 454A. One additional 4Q4 was needed at DG to cover this change.

On 8th November, the 342 (New Barnet-Hertford) was extended to Broxbourne replacing the withdrawn 380A. Three 5Q5s were used from HG. Until this date, the 342 had been jointly scheduled with 303/A whose requirement now became four 5Q5 from HF daily. From 13th December the Hertford-Buntingford circular route 331 reduced its allocation from three to two 5Q5s on Monday to Friday from HG. Then on 19th December, route 340 was withdrawn and most of it was augmented by the strengthened 341 which was converted to STL at the same time. One 5Q5 was saved at both HG and HF.

Increasing capacity by replacing saloons by deckers was an on-going theme where it was possible. And now it was the larger capacity STL rather than the ST, most of which were out of service, which was used. This had happened to the 415 on 18th October when two 4Q4s were replaced by STLs at GF. On 17th January 1940, it was the turn of the 455 whose schedule was separated from the 305 and needed two STLs allowing HE to release Q81/9 to MA. 305

was withdrawn between Beaconsfield and High Wycombe and was operated by two 4Q4s from MA.

7th February 1940 saw some reorganisation to the St Albans services. 355 was withdrawn between St Albans and Harpenden so that its requirement reduced from SA five 4Q4 to three 5Q5s (with an instruction to include a 341 fare table). OMO Cub route 391 was expanded to replace part of the 355 with a new section introduced between Hill End and Harpenden as well as its previous routing between Tyttenhanger and St Albans with Saturday pm journeys to Sandridge. At weekends part of 391A was also diverted to serve Tyttenhanger. The weekend 365 was diverted in St Albans to terminate at at Hill End. Joint scheduling from SA was now 4Q4 10/11/9. A fare table on one of the Qs was needed for trunk route 321. 355 used three 5Q5s. Incidentally, SA's 354 had replaced its two 4Q4s with a pair of Ts. From 18th February the Ware Park Sanatorium Sunday only service 349 replaced its 4Q4 with an STL from SA.

The schedule for 13th March 1940 contains a number of other small adjustments affecting the Q class over the period. Route 312 increased its 4Q4 requirement from two to three at WA. RG's 406C was now needed to carry fare charts for trunk route 405 as well as the 427. The 434 at EG increased its 4Q4 allocation from two to three. Meanwhile the Pinewood Studios routes 457B/C used only one Monday to Friday 4Q4 ex WR instead of two.

The trend to double decking continued where possible. The first route to be converted was 311/A at WA which replaced its four 4Q4s with STLs. Three of these, STL 1487/92 1521 were transferred from Tunbridge Wells (TW) on 12th March when temporary route 403D was replaced by reinstatement of Green Line C. These were forward entrance Weymann bodied l/6STL6/1s.

On 1st May, 331 was converted from three 5Q5s to two STLs and one 5Q5. STLl179,1788 in red livery were transferred from Chelverton Road (AF) where they were replaced by brand new 2RT2s. At this time, HG had been receiving a handful of red STLs from AF.

On 30th July, STl117 was transferred to EG from MA. This was used to convert route 428, although Q93 did not leave EG until 28th August.

On 14th May, Q98/9 were transferred from MA to GD for the 410 (Bromley-Reigate). Initially one was used but from 26th May, the route was split into two unconnected sections: Reigate-Biggin Hill and Bromley-Leaves Green. Both 4Q4s were then needed. However, from 10th July, the Bromley-Leaves Green section was converted to three STLs from DG, and officially the Qs were no longer scheduled. Q99

moved on to SA that day but Q98 remained until 25th September, when it moved to WY. The reason for the upheaval to the route was brought about as a result of the security surrounding Biggin Hill Airfield.

On 21st May the Pinewood Studios routes 457B/C were withdrawn. The 4Q4 saved was then added to the 457/A allocation at WR.

Throughout the period there were adjustments at SA and HG which included another shunting of 5Q5s. On 27th March, Q164/5 were transferred from SA to HG, their place at SA being taken by Q94 ex EG and Q85 ex NF. Q159 moved from SA to HF on 1st May. Route 355 at SA once again reverted to 4Q4s. On 31st July, HG's requirement on the 342 reduced from three to two 5Q5s.

Several of the former Green Line l/4Q4/ls were reallocated for work as duplicates on Green Line services some of which had been reinstated earlier in the year. Q98 ex GD, Q92 ex RG, Q82 ex WR moved to WY for these duties on the C (Tunbridge Wells-Chertsey). However from 23rd October, the route was split into two sections, and the buses worked on the western section between Chertsey and Victoria alongside the scheduled 10T10s. The 5Q5s with their open front entrance were not available for Green Line reliefs and their use was restricted to certain Country Area bus routes, whilst the 1/4Q4/1s were the preferred type for coach duplicates as they had kept their luggage racks.

The Blitz commenced in earnest in September 1940, and with the lengthening evenings and potential damage to the railways, the Government authorised the restoration of much of the Green Line network in December. There were no cross-London routes, and both existing services which had resumed earlier in the year and all other Green Line reinstatements received route numbers rather than letters. The first stage of the restoration took place on 4th December.

All the 6Q6s were needed for ambulance work, and it was the T class Regals which bore the brunt of this work – especially 10T10s. It was necessary, however, to use l/4Q4/ls at HE for the 33 (formerly Q) (High Wycombe-Oxford Circus), at MA for 34 (formerly R) (Chesham/Amersham-Oxford Circus), and at Hertford for 49 (formerly M) (Hertford-Oxford Circus). This involved a considerable upheaval for the class.

MA received Q93 104/5 ex DG, Q82 ex WR, Q83 ex GF, Q20,80 ex WY and Q88,91 ex RG for the 34 which required eight scheduled buses.

HE received Q66,86/7,92/8, 100/86/7 ex WY for 33 which required seven scheduled buses.

HG received Q84 ex NF and Q85,94-7/9, 101-3 ex SA for 49 which required ten scheduled buses.

There were various knock-on effects. Q170/2/5 moved from HG to SA to convert the 355 to 5Q5s yet again.

Q15,24/6 ex WR, and Q22 ex WY, were transferred into SA to cover for the losses to HG. Q79 went from RG to NF. Q66 which had moved into HE was needed to cover an increase from 5 to 6 Qs on 353 group. The 406C and 440 both from RG were converted to T, as indeed had been the WSSu operation of 382. DG's workings on 454/A were similarly revised to use Ts. WT however regained 4Q4s after some time without: Q44,54/8/9 arrived from WY and these were used on what had previously been T duties, so that the Regals could fit in elsewhere. WR and WY had lost virtually all of their 4Q4s.

During the preceding weeks, London Transport had received a substantial number of loans of provincial buses from all over the country. The buses were of a great variety of types and initially they had been allocated mainly to Central Area garages on an ad hoc basis. The opportunity was taken after a few weeks to sort these out by type and the single-deckers were allocated to Country Area garages. Dennises (mainly Lancet models) were allocated to both WR and WY to cover for the buses transferred elsewhere. Examples came from Eastern Counties, Eastern National, North Western Road Car Co and West Yorkshire Road Car Co and worked the 335, 436/A,457/A,461/A and part of 462 in place of the 4Q4s.

The second phase of the reorganisation took place on 18th December. Route 34 (MA) and 33 (HE) had proved so busy that they were converted to double-deckers using STs, most of them red, which had just been reinstated to service. The l /4Q4/ls from HE and MA were reallocated. GD received Q91/3 from MA and Q98, 100 ex HE. EG got Q86/7/90/2 ex HE, and GF got Q186/7 ex HE. Q86/7/90/2 moved from MA to HG. They were all needed for duplicates. On 18th December, HE's route 455A was converted to STL. The displaced 4Q4, Q30, was transferred out to WT on Christmas Day.

1941–1943

The Country Area Qs proved just as restless in 1941. During the earlier period the year records show that the reinstated Green Line network was proving so popular that 60 duplicates were required Monday to Friday, 110 on Saturday and an amazing 140 on Sunday. Of course, these were drawn from across the fleet but the Qs played a major role. In some cases, they were allocated to garages not normally associated with either the route or indeed Green Line work at all. By the summer with the use of double-deckers on some routes, the demand for duplicates declined to some extent, but there was still plentiful work at weekends. It is a reflection of how adaptable these solid workhorses were that they could perform equally well on lengthy limited stop services to Central London as they could on short routes such as the 387 in Tring or along the country lanes of Surrey.

In the first few weeks of 1941, Q91/3/5,100 left GD for WY, indeed the first two were swapped with a couple of North Western petrol engined Dennises.

On 17th February, LT1427/8 were reinstated to service and allocated to SA where they partially converted the 355 from 5Q5 to LTL. At least these were in green livery. More surprising two days later was the transfer of red LT1040/4/70 from Sutton (A) to WA where they converted the 312 from 4Q4 to the type. (This was to be short-lived as, from 13th August, 312 was converted to STs). The next day LT1080 moved from A to HG to begin the conversion of the 342. The route had to wait until 30th April, before this bus was joined by LT1175 and LT1200, also from A, to complete the conversion. The three displaced 5Q5s converted two services new to the type, the 350/A both linking Hertford with Bishops Stortford.

2nd April 1941 saw a programme of route changes. The trend to the use of double-deckers continued wherever that was possible. 303/A were converted to STL, and 5Q5s Q166/9/73/8 moved from HF to SA. Route 354 then returned to using 5Q5s ex Ts. Route 331, which had been using two STLs and one 5Q5, was fully double-decked now using three STs.

In the Southern Area, the scheduling of the 429 was detached from the 439, and was converted to ST at DS. One single-decker was still required, at first a provincial bus, but in June, spare 5Q5s Q166/9 were allocated to DS from SA. The 439 now required two 4Q4s from RG.

At this time, RG received Q17,32,55,69,79 from NF, and transferred six Ts to LH. LH then sent six Bristol Tramways & Carriage Co oil AEC Regals to NF where they took over from Qs on 489 and 497. RG was now able to return Q operation to routes 427 and 440. Route 418 was extended from Effingham to Guildford at this time replacing route 432 over this section. The requirement became LH 7/8/8 and GF 2/2/2. However, the initial operation of the route was with Ts. 418A retained 4Q4s with LH continuing to borrow from RG to make up the four bus requirement on Sundays. At this same time, the two buses on GF's 438 became 5Q5, ex 4Q4 with the arrival of Q159/62.

Services in the Watford and Hemel Hempstead area were reorganised at this time and the 307 Group was jointly scheduled. The routes concerned were 307 (Harpenden-Chesham), 318 (Watford-Chipperfield), 320 and 322 (Watford-Hemel Hempstead), the new 322A, which was 325 renumbered (Abbots Langley-Hemel Hempstead), and new 322B (also Abbots Langley-Hemel Hempstead). Variation in intermediate routings was the reason for the use of different numbers for the same pair of termini. At this date, the scheduling for the entire group was HH T 9/9/7 and WT 4Q4 4/4/5. Journeys were also worked on a substantial number of other routes: 301,302,307A,317,319,337,377/A/B,378 and 391.

Throughout the spring the routes at WY and WR which had been using provincial Dennises were slowly converted back to Qs as the borrowed buses were withdrawn and Qs became available. However, 461A and 462 received Ts rather than the Qs which had operated prior to the loans.

On 30th April, ST129/52 arrived at MA to convert the 306. Although nominally this had been a 4Q4 route, red T6,24 departed for Sidcup (SP).

T639/40/4/7/81/91/700 were transferred from Tunbridge Wells (TW) to MA on 14th June to convert Green Line 35 (Aylesbury-Victoria) which although officially 7T7 had in fact been using 4Q4s. Q65/7,81,97/9 then moved across to WR replacing loaned Dennises. Following from this, the 10T10s at NF for Green Line route 2 were displaced when it was converted to STL. T616/9/21-4/38/49/88/9, 715 moved across to HG to replace the last 4Q4s on frontline Green Line service 49.

Through the later part of June, the spare Qs at HG moved to WY, HF and SA. Opportunity was also taken to withdraw loaned Dermises at WY and GD, and United Auto Bristols at HG itself including the one bus on the 329A. EG withdrew from Green Line relief duties and Q86/7,90/2 were transferred to WR.

On 9th July, 457/A at WR were converted to STL continuing the strategy of using bigger buses wherever possible. The allocation was nominally four 4Q4s at that date although only Q16,27 were transferred out to HF whilst two West Yorkshire Dennis Lancets were withdrawn. Over at SA on the same day, the 354 was converted from two 5Q5s to two STs.

On 13th August the six Bristol Regals at NF were withdrawn from the 489 and 497. Q16,57,61 replaced them from HF, and Q31,40,99 from WR. The Qs from HF were replaced by a mixed collection: STL960/7, 1024 together with T540 ex SA. This latter bus was replaced by Q27 ex HF and Q103 ex WA which more than covered the one bus requirement on the Wednesday, Saturday, Sunday 382 to Codicote.

Further changes followed on 8th October. 350/A, the Bishops Stortford services were converted to ST thus displacing the three 5Q5s. In fact Q164/8/71/7 moved from HG to RG for the revamped 447 which

had been extended to Redhill covering for 427 which had been withdrawn the previous day. One 4Q4 was needed additionally to cover the five bus allocation which also included 447A and 447B. (Q1 continued to provide yeoman service at the garage.)

On the same day, 416 (Leatherhead-Esher) was converted from OMO Cub to crewed 4Q4, Q61 being transferred to LH ex NF for the purpose. Three spare 4Q4s around the fleet were also used to convert 461A from T to 4Q4 at WY – Q49 ex SA, Q97 ex WR and Q105 ex MA.

On 13th October, Q167/70 were transferred from SA to Luton (LS). 5Q5s were clearly not popular there as on 25th November they were exchanged with Q15/9 from SA. It may have been that the 4Q4s were more flexible being able to work Green Line reliefs. The Allocation Book is silent on what use the 5Q5s may have been put. 356/A, 364/A and 376/ A all used Ts, and were possible candidates.

Throughout this period, many garages had allocations of buses well over and above the scheduled requirement together with a prudent cover for spares. Some of the additional vehicles were needed for private contracts and, in particular, for moving the work forces of factories, many of national importance, which were located away from the vulnerable capital city which was suffering so badly during the Blitz. Even though both local and Green Line services had their capacity increased with the use of double-deckers, duplicates and reliefs were still needed, and were worked according to local instruction. Before, and indeed after the War, it is possible to relate bus movements to route and/ or schedule changes closely, but there are often discrepancies between the scheduled requirement and the number of buses allocated during these dark days of war. On the face of it, the 4Q4s and Country 5Q5s appear to be underemployed as a result of various double-decker conversions, but in reality this was far from the case.

DG was the next garage to exchange its Ts for 4Q4s. On 26th November, Q55 moved in from RG, and on 4th December, Q8, 25 and 60 arrived from HE. Two were needed for 454/A, and the other two were used on 431 and the new 431A, a weekday works service between Sevenoaks and Orpington which was introduced on 22nd December.

At this time the Government had authorised the completion of buses which had been halted in build as a result of priorities elsewhere. STL2648-81 were thirty-four AEC Regents which received a mixture of new Chiswick-built bodies and second-hand ones taken from float. These "unfrozen" buses were classified 17STLs, and were especially suited to the hilly routes operated by MA and HE. They were all delivered in Central Area red livery, and a substantial proportion was used to convert routes 353,362/A/B and 366 from a mixture of STs and 4Q4s.

The first four, STL 2648/9/52/69, were allocated to HE on 1st December. They continued to enter service throughout the month and Qs were displaced from HE as follows: 1/12 Q66 to SA, 4/12 QS,25,60 to DG, 17/12 Q33 to GF, 1/1/42 Q62 to RG, and finally 14/2 Q35 to SA. The scheduled requirement had been six 4Q4s.

The first 17STLs to enter service at MA were STL2659/70 on 1st January 1942. Delivery continued until 1st June when STL2671 was licensed. The buses were used to replace eight 4Q4s and four STs. The 4Q4s were displaced as follows: 1/1 Q64,71 to SA, 12/1 Q39 to GD, 5/2 Q12 to GD, Q28 to WY, Q68 to SA, 1/3 Q80, 105 to SA, and 25/3 Q20,104 to HF.

On 8th December 1941, Q92 had its capacity altered with the introduction of perimeter seating of 32, and a standing area for a further twenty passengers at peak times. At the same time it was reallocated from WR to WY. The programme continued throughout 1942, and indeed the last example, Q45 was dealt with in June 1943. Only fifteen of the 4Q4s were not dealt with.

With the use of double-deckers on some Green Line routes as well as the conversion to an upper deck on other Country routes, there was a slight decrease in demand for single-deckers. On 13th January 1942, 5Q5s Q174 ex GF was replaced by 4Q4 Q33, ex HE, and Q168 ex RG replaced by Q62, ex HE. The two buses were painted red and transferred to the central Area at Sidcup (SP) where demand on route 241, a service where single-deckers were essential, was outstripping capacity. Then in March Q151/9/62/7/70/2/5 all SA buses were painted red and transferred to Dalston (D). They were replaced at SA by Q68,80,105 ex MA, Q35,40 ex HE, and Q6,11,49 ex WA. These however proved the limit to what the Country Department felt could be released at that time.

In January 1942, works journeys on 431/A were converted to double-decker from DG. These were other services where factories en route created surges in demand. Some of the deckers worked off the 402 and 410.

On 4th March, route 335 (Watford and Windsor via The Chalfonts) was converted to double-deck. ST1102/2 7 were allocated to WA whose 4Q4s went to SA replacing 5Q5s, and STL988, 1443 were transferred to WR. Q65/7 then moved from here to HG for route 342 which now needed two 4Q4s replacing 5Q5s, and the one LTL which continued as before.

9th June was the date of the next set of changes, this time affecting routes 416 and 418/A. 416 was converted from 4Q4 to double-decker using ST1039 ex Romford (RE). (The route had grown from Cub to decker via 4Q4 in a very short time.) 418/A were mainly converted to Q ex T, their requirement being LH 4Q4 8/9/12 (including some Ts), and GF 4Q4 2/2/2.

GF received Q19 ex LS, the latter garage replacing its small allocation of Qs with Ts, and Q105 ex SA. (Q34 at LS moved to SA at the same time). LH which absorbed the bus from 416 received Q10/1 ex SA, and Q47,69,76 ex RG. The RG buses were replaced by T549/51,603 at the same time.

Throughout that summer, 309, 357/A at WT were in the process of a slow conversion from T to 4Q4. On 18th July, Q45,67 arrived from HG, whilst T284/94 went in the opposite direction converting the 342 to the class. In the following weeks, Q12,20, 103 all moved in from SA.

On 30th September 1942, and for the second time, all Green Line services were withdrawn. This action was taken despite their heavy patronage as a way of conserving fuel and resources during some of the darkest days of the War years. Certain bus services were altered to take account of the losses. 357/A, the so-called 'Northwood Services' were withdrawn, although partially covered by an extension of 345 and 346 from Northwood to Harefield. 355 was extended from Radlett to Borehamwood to provide a partial replacement of 311A and Green Line 45. The two 4Q4s, Q6,20 saved at WT from 357/A, moved to SA where the allocation on the 355 increased to five Qs from a mixture of Qs and LTLs.

Over at RG route 439 was converted from 4Q4 to T. One notable withdrawal at the garage was that of the Q prototype, Q1. At the same time, 449 at GD lost Qs for Ts.

A substantial proportion of the entire fleet was delicensed in this latest round of austerity, and the 4Q4s did not escape. The buses involved included Q52,85 HFu, Q63,78,186 MAu, Q42,56,75 GDu, Q22,35/7 SAu, Q84 100 WYu, and Q1,13,69,76 RGu. Opportunity was not taken to transfer the 5Q5s to the Central Area, and replace them with the delicensed 4Q4s at the time.

On 1st November 1942, Q45,56 and 75 were reinstated at GD, and Q18 and Q84 at RG. Routes 449 and 439 returned to Q operation. Then followed a very quiet winter as far as the class was concerned. But on 1st March 1943, Q22,37,63,78 were reinstated at Hemel Hempstead (HH), a garage which had operated virtually none of the class before, and they were put to work on the 307 group of services.

In fact on 3rd March routes 322A and 322B were withdrawn, and 318A was introduced between Watford and Two Waters. Apart from 307 itself, 307A, 318 and 320 continued as before. WT had been using 4Q4s for some time and the allocation for the group was WT 4Q4 4/4/5 and HH 4Q4 4/4/4 and T 11/8/3. Journeys were operated on various other local routes including the 377 group with 377A, 377B and 378 covering works journeys to Apsley Mills.

The programme of conversion to perimeter seating allowing twenty standees for the 4Q4s continued until June 1943 when, with the alteration to Q45, it stopped. Q13/7,22,37,63,75/8, 81/4/6-8, 91/8, 100 remained B35C throughout. Routes needed to be licensed individually for this type of peak standee operation.

During August 1942, nine 4Q4s were painted in a camouflage grey livery. Q17,18,40 and 86 were allocated to RG, and Q8,15,28,39 and 61 were at WY where they worked on the Vickers Works services. In June 1943, Q8 and 28 were transferred to HH for works services.

Q15 saw operation from GF for the first two weeks of December 1943. Q173 and Q177 were the only 5Q5s to be painted grey, and operated from RG on the 440 and 447 throughout. All the grey Qs regained their green livery in the autumn and winter of 1944-45, Q173 being the very last on 20th February 1945

It will be useful to summarise the results of all these changes by reference to the Allocation of Scheduled Buses (No. 13) for 5th May 1943.

Even at the time of this schedule, changes were afoot. At the end of April, STL2,90,1880 and 2119 were transferred from SA to HH where they took up duties mainly on the busy Apsley Mills services, and effectively converted route 378 to double-deck. On 1st May, T267/9/75,361/2 were transferred from HH to HG where 342 was converted from 4Q4 to T. During May Q76,83,187 then moved from HG to SA to replace three Ts which had temporarily been providing single-decker support.

On 1st June, the Ts at HH were delicensed being replaced by 4Q4s: Q8,9,28,94/5/7 from WY and Q85,186 being reinstated. Q8 and 28 were in camouflage grey livery and were no doubt useful on the routes serving the strategically important Bovingdon Airfield. Two further works services were introduced at this time: 318B/C (Two Waters-Chipperfield/Kings Langley). They were worked from the pool of buses for the 307 group and were specified for single-deckers.

1st June also saw a reorganisation of the WY services again with the aim of increasing capacity wherever

possible with double-deckers. Route 436 was split at Woking with the Staines-Woking section being converted to lowbridge STL. The three buses, STL2229,2291 and 2311 had new Chiswick-built lowbridge bodies painted in the camouflage grey livery, and indeed STL2311, which was licensed on 10th June 1943, was notable in being the last ever mainstream new body built there, other than the odd repair and experimental one. Route 436A was shortened to work between Woking and Ripley, and the 436 between Guildford and Woking retained the GF allocation using three 4Q4s daily.

461/A were both split at Walton. Walton-Addlestone (461), and Walton-Ottershaw (461A) were converted to grey STs working with producer gas, ST47,192,324/35,648,730,801 being allocated on that day. 461B was amended to run between Walton and Vickers Works with journeys to Hersham, and a new 456B circular weekday works service was introduced serving Addlestone, Byfleet and Vickers Works. In both cases, camouflaged single-deckers were mainly used although certain STs were instructed to carry fare charts for odd journeys on both routes. The rump of 461 between Hersham and Walton now used two 4Q4s from WY daily. There were other alterations to routes in the area, but as they did not involve the Q class they are omitted here.

There were no other significant changes for six months, and the next set of adjustments occurred later in December. Route 439 was amended to operate between Redhill and Newdigate, and the opportunity was taken to convert it to double-decker inter-working with the 429. The remaining service between Reigate and Merstham was numbered 439A, and this was inter-worked with the 449 the joint scheduling now becoming GD 4Q4 3/3/3, and RG 4Q4 1/1/1. RG was able to send its surplus bus, Q56 to EG and Q87,98 were licensed at EG from store at the same time to cover the enhancements to the 424 which doubled its Q requirement to six.

Enhancements to the 355 at SA also required two extra Qs, and Q84/8 were taken from store. Cub route 304 (Hillend-Whitwell/Hitchin) now used a 4Q4 on weekdays for its busier St Albans to Kimpton shorts.

1944–1949

Both 1944 and 1945 were to prove to be two of the quieter years as far as the Qs were concerned. Nonetheless, on the very first day of 1944, routes 431/A were converted to STL, STL1488, 1502/12 moving across from WA to DG, where they were replaced by reinstated STs. Q55/60 were transferred to EG, and Q73 to GF.

On 5th April, there were further adjustments to the "307 Group". 307 itself was withdrawn between

Chesham and Boxmoor so that it now worked between Harpenden and Boxmoor only. 316 was introduced between Chesham and Hemel Hempstead, in the main using STs. 317 (Watford-Berkhamsted) and 337 (Watford-Dunstable) were incorporated into the complicated pattern of workings within the group. 317A was withdrawn and 318 (Chipperfield-Watford) was extended beyond Watford to Sarratt absorbing it. 318A (Two Waters-Watford) was extended to Bucks Hill absorbing the 347. Finally 320 (Watford-Hemel Hempstead) was extended to Boxmoor. The schedule now became: HH 4Q4 12/12/10, T 2/2/0, ST 4/2/2, STL 2/2/0, WT 4Q4 6/6/6, T 1/1/0, STL 2/4/0 and WA STL 0/3/0. The only Q movement was the transfer of Q9 and 57 from HH to WT.

The support of the T class was somewhat fluid at both garages, as indeed it was throughout where garages used Qs. By 17th May, 309 increased its 4Q4 requirement at WT to 7/8/9 ex 5/6/7. 377 was temporarily withdrawn at that date. On 1st July, Q100 was reinstated to HH and on 1st September Q71,95 joined it, so that in theory the Ts were eliminated. On 11th August, Q87/8 were reinstated at WT to take account of the increased requirement of 8/10/4 4Q4s together with a T each day. On 1st October Q98 was transferred to TG so that 387 now used two Qs instead of one Q and one T. This only lasted until 16th February 1945 when it was replaced by T622.

The position in the southern area was even quieter. 418/A increased its Monday-Friday need by one Q at LH, whilst there were small adjustments to 425 5Q5 allocations at GF and DS.

On 1st January 1945 Q37 and 68 were allocated to CY replacing the pair of Ts on route 426 (Crawley-Charlwood-Horley-Crawley). On 4th April, ST218 and 393 were reinstated at NF to convert 497 to double-decker. In the event this double-decking did not last and Ts replaced them from 28th August 1946. In the changes of 6th February 1946, 489 had been organised to run between Singlewell and Gravesend covering for part of the 490, and new route 489A was introduced between Gravesend and Northumberland Bottom covering part of 451.

Most of the transfers of the 4Q4s were brought about as a result of the class going through a fifth overhaul cycle during the period. It is often forgotten that during the War buses still needed regular attention and although the overhauls, most of which took place at garages rather than centrally, may not have been as thorough as during peacetime, London Transport could not afford to let its buses fall into disrepair as the resultant unreliability would have been self-defeating. The period between overhauls for the 4Q4s had extended from about eighteen months to two years. In November 1945 the replacement of the perimeter seating by the previous B35C layout began in earnest, and continued throughout the winter, and this eliminated the space for twenty standees which had been allowed under the emergency conditions.

Ts continued to be used on Q routes as stopgaps. A short-lived episode occurred on 27th November 1945, when the two 4Q4s at DG on 454/A were replaced by T555,575 and 653. For whatever reason, this was not a success, and on 10th December, T555 moved out to HG, and T575 to HH, Q18 and Q25 returning to DG. A small improvement occurred at SA on 5th December when route 382 which had worked only on Wednesday, Saturday and Sunday was provided with a daily service. One 4Q4 was sufficient.

1946 saw the staged return of Green Line services commencing 6th February and they were numbered in the seven hundred series. The Green Line 6Q6s were converted back from ambulances to coaches and played their part. Routes employing them initially were: 709 (Caterham-Baker St), 710 (Crawley-Baker St), 711 (Reigate-Baker St), 724 (High Wycombe-Oxford Circus), and 725 (Chesham-Oxford Circus). The garages were GD, CY, RG, HE and MA respectively. In June, 715 (Guildford-Hertford) swapped its 10T10s for the 6Q6s on 709, 710 and 711 so that coach Qs worked from GF and HG instead of GD, CY and RG.

By 10th July, thirty-nine 6Q6s were allocated to Green Line routes on Monday to Friday out of a total of forty-nine. Q217 had been destroyed by enemy action at Elmers End (ED) garage on 18th July 1944, the only member of single-deck Qs to suffer such a wartime fate.

Traffic built up quickly especially at weekends, and once again a substantial number of duplicates was required, including where available, 4Q4s. Just before the re-introduction of the coach network, Q100, the only 1/4Q4/1 which had not been converted back to a bus, entered service at SA on 8th January wearing an experimental all green livery complete with Green Line transfers.

One other item of note occurred on 23rd January 1946 when Q1 which had been in store for many months was sold to a dealer. It was accompanied by C1. What a shame that the preservation movement was still many years away!

On 16th January the 418 was amended to operate between Kingston and Preston Cross, and 418A between West Ewell and Preston Cross. The routes were double-decked using ten STs from LH daily. Two new routes were introduced to cover the remaining sections: 419 (West Ewell-Epsom Clock Tower), and 432 (Guildford-Great Bookham). The 419 allocation was LH 4Q4 2/2/2 with three Ts on Sunday, and 432 was GF 4Q4 2/2/2 with one LH T on Monday to Friday. From 29th May, 419 was extended from Epsom to Langley Vale and in the course of doing so lost one 4Q4 but gained two 10T10s. It was not until 1st February that QI0/1,29,32 and 47 were delicensed at LH.

During the spring there were several unusual and short-lived allocations of the odd Q to garages not normally associated with them. They were not scheduled for specific duties. Q30 at Epping (EP) from 12th to 19th March. Q39,61 at Windsor (WR) from 27th March to 29th May. Q10 at Staines (ST) from 8th April to 7th May.

Further changes in the southern area took place on 1st May. To make room for the allocation of Green Line route 708 at EG, the duties on 434 were transferred to CY which now became CY 4Q4 4/3/2. This was increased to CY 4Q4 6/6/5 from 12th June. There was also one STL daily. Q70/2/7 moved from EG to CY on 1st May. At the same time 424 increased its requirement by one 4Q4 to seven at EG.

Route 449 was withdrawn, and 447 was extended to Woldingham. The 439A now used a bus from 447/A/B allocation which had become RG 5Q5 6/6/6 and 4Q4 4/4/1. Q40/5, 101 moved from GD to RG while Q98 went from GD to SA. Additionally 440 was withdrawn betwee·n S Merstham and Redhill Station. New route 440A was introduced on 29th May between Redhill Station and Redstone Estate. There was a joint schedule with the 440 which became RG 4Q4 2/2/1.

The 307 group mopped up any spare Qs so that by 2nd October the requirement was HH 4Q4 12/11/8 and WT 4Q4 11/11/6.

1947 was a particularly difficult year for the Board. Passenger demand was soaring at a time when older dilapidated buses were having to be withdrawn, and orders, especially for the new RT were delayed by shortages, tooling up problems, and a lack of skilled labour. The winter of 1946/47 was one of the coldest and most severe of the century and there were the added difficulties of repairing the knocks sustained on the icy roads.

Such was the shortage of serviceable buses that the Country Area was unable to operate the expected enhancements of a summer programme. This was all the more unpopular when the summer turned out to be a glorious one after the bad winter. No revised allocation schedule was issued in June, and planned service improvements either were shelved, or had to wait until the autumn. Even then, things were not straightforward. The changes, many of which were affected by the reduction of the standard working week for crew from 48 to 44 hours, which had been planned for 29th October did not take place until 12th November.

Demand for the Green Line was buoyant, and duplicates had been provided wherever possible. There was a surplus of l0Tl0 coaches in particular and these were used for both reliefs and for normal bus work. On 1st September, there was a large delicensing programme affecting most classes including the Qs: Q20,35,46,64,98 and 102 at SA, Q28,52,68 a HH, Q17, 86 at RG, Q169 at DS and Q178 at GF. This shortfall at SA in particular was covered by 9T9s on route 355.

The major changes occurred on 12th November. The 1946 alterations on routes 489/A were reversed with 489 withdrawn between Gravesend and Singlewell, and 489A withdrawn between Gravesend and Northumberland Bottom and diverted to Hook Green. Frequencies were increased with the requirement becoming NF 4Q4 3/3/3.

The complicated scheduling of the 307 group was split although a great deal of cross-working continued to take place. The revised schedules became: 307/A HH 4Q4 2/2/2, WT 4Q4 0/1/0, 316 HH ST 2/2/2, 317 HH T 2/2/2, 318/A, 320 WT 4Q4 9/7/6, HH 4Q4 7/5/2, 322 HH 4Q4 3/3/3, WT 4Q4 2/2/0, 337 HH 4Q4 1/1/1, WT 4Q4 0/1/0. On Monday to Friday, HH needed a total of thirteen 4Q4s, and WT eleven 4Q4s. Q47,61 were transferred into WT, and Q29,105 into HH on this date.

At EG, 424 was strengthened further to 4Q4 8/7/7 and Q7 was the additional bus.

Changes to the Green Line network had a knock-on effect. Routes 724 and 725 were withdrawn, and replaced by extending the Baker Street routes northward. 709 now ran to Chesham over the former 725 roads, and 710 worked to Amersham. Seven additional buses were required at MA for these services, and the 6Q6s were replaced by 10Tl0s so that the allocation by type was standardised with those from the southern garages. T620 ex HH, and T617/24/9/64/7/91 ex DG made up the numbers. 711 was extended from Baker Street to High Wycombe via the old 724, and again the 6Q6s at HE were replaced by T537,684,716 ex WT, T613 ex HH, T675 ex WY, T512 ex EG, and T616, 713 ex NF.

The 6Q6s, which had spent the entire war years as ambulances in the Central Area, had lower mileages than the 4Q4s, and it was decided that the displaced coaches should be used on Country Area bus routes. Q212/3/22/3/6 were transferred from MA to SA for the 355 which then took on the distinction of having worked 4Q4s,5Q5s and 6Q6s. Q202 and Q218 were relicensed to SA a few days later. The official allocation was SA 6Q6 7/7/7 and 4Q4 0/1/0.

T41l/25-7/41/7, 9T9s which had temporarily made up the shortfall at SA, moved to DG thus releasing 10T10s to MA. The balance of the spare 6Q6s moved to GF where they replaced 4Q4s on routes 432, 6Q6 2/2/2, 436A 6Q6 1/1/1, and 438 6Q6 2/2/2. In addition, the single-deck section of 436 running between Guildford and Woking was renumbered 436B and required 6Q6 3/3/3. Q189/91 200/5/7 /9/10/28 came from HE. The displaced 4Q4s moved from GF to EG (Q7), RG (Q23,38), WT (Q47,61) and HH (Q29,105).

The Monday to Friday requirement for Qs had altered markedly over the year.

	31/12/1946	31/12/1947
4Q4	87	70
5Q5	12	12
6Q6 Bus	0	16
6Q6 Coach	43	28

The real shortages were of double-deckers both in the Central and the Country area. Indeed, on 30th April 1948 Q29,32 and 55 moved into Swanley (SJ) to work the 478 (Swanley-Wrotham) which had used ST and STLs. (This however was short-lived, and the Qs were swapped for Ts on 20th May). The Country Department was allocated thirty brand new AEC Regals with handsome Mann Egerton bodies during the year, T769-798, the last new buses to be delivered in the old livery of dark green and white. It was decided that they should be allocated to just two garages, eighteen to HH and 12 to WT where they gradually displaced 4Q4s, and a few older Ts. The new buses were classified 15T13s, the first one, T769, entering service on 6th March 1948.

The time had clearly come when the remaining green 5Q5s could be sent to the Central Area where they had originally been intended to operate. On 13th April, Q163 was transferred from RG to Sidcup (SP) where it worked in green livery for a year before it was repainted red. On 15th July, Q152/66/73/5/7 were painted red and reallocated from GF to SP. Next day, Q176/8 were treated in exactly the same way, and Q164 followed on 21st. This last bus had been allocated to RG.

On 3rd August, Q169 (ex DS), and Q171/80/2 (ex RG) were transferred to Cricklewood (W) where they provided transport for the Olympic Games that month still in their green livery. When these special duties were completed, they also moved to SP and were soon in red livery. This left just Q155 and 179 both formerly at GF which were painted red in August and joined their brothers at SP. The 447 group of routes at RG were able to use 4Q4s displaced by the 15T13s at HH and WT. 4Q4s and 6Q6s were prohibited from working route 425, so both GF and DS converted to 10T10s for this service.

Such was the demand for single-deckers in the Central Area on busy routes that the transfer of Country Qs did not stop there. On 11th August, Q8,53 and 67 were painted red and transferred to West Green (WG) for route 233. Q44 and 68 followed later in the month.

Operation on the 233 was not successful. The platform doors had to be roped open to comply with Police Regulations, and the drivers complained about the poor nearside vision.

After a few weeks, the 4Q4s were transferred to Dalston (D). In September, Q65 and in October, Q85 were also painted red and allocated straight to D. Although further transfers had originally been planned, dissatisfaction with the operation of 4Q4s in the Central Area put a halt for the moment to this process.

Q85 was the only 1/4Q4/1 to be involved in this procedure. It will be recalled that at the end of 1936 seven 4Q4s had also been painted red and allocated to Cricklewood (W) and Kingston (K), but these allocations lasted for only a few weeks.

One noteworthy event occurred on 25th June 1948 when Q100 at SA was at last converted from Green Line coach to an ordinary bus, which had happened to all the other 14Q4/1s prior to the War.

On 25th March, Q7 moved into Chelsham (CM), a garage which had never worked the class before. On 20th May, a substantial allocation followed: Q11,20 ex SA, Q12/5 ex WT, Q28,52,71,105 ex HH, Q29,32,55 ex SJ and Q44 ex EP. Some were used to convert the 453 (Warlingham Green-Caterham-on-the-Hill) from T to 4Q4. But the majority were used on specific sections of trunk routes which otherwise used double-deckers. Some were stop-gaps until new RTs could be allocated. Although 4Q4s could not work the 403 (Tonbridge-Wallington) from end to end, three were employed to increase the frequency on the busy section between West Croydon and Beddington. They also appeared on 403A (Wallington-Warlingham Park Hospital) and 403E (Wallington-Farleigh). Although they were not officially scheduled, there is ample photographic evidence for this.

On 30th June, the shorts on 403 were withdrawn, and replaced by a frequency increase on the double-deck 408 (Chelsham-Guildford) between West Croydon and Epsom. Six additional 4Q4 were needed for this. A frequency increase on 453 brought that allocation to CM 4Q4 3/3/1.

It will be observed that Q44 had moved into CM from Epping (EP) where it had been since going there from HH on 14th April. It was replaced on 27th May by Q95 which stayed until 29th September. There was no official scheduled working, but it most likely operated on 399 (Hertford-Coopersale Street) whose requirement was EP T 2/2/1. The 399 was part of the 308 group of services which also used Ts from Hertford (HG) and Hitchin (HN).

It will be useful one again to summarise the duties of the Q class in the County Area.

Despite the shortage of serviceable single-deckers in the Central Area, the red 4Q4s were soon returned: Q44,53,65/7 in February and Q8,68,85 in March 1949. Q67 and 68 were repainted green in April and August respectively but the rest worked in their red livery. Q8,53,68 and 85 went to TG. Two were used on the 387 which had temporarily slipped back into T operation whilst two were used on double-deck trunk route 301 for the short workings between Tring and Aylesbury. At least the red buses did not come near any Central Area routes to cause confusion.

The March programme saw a slight adjustment at WT. Three of the six 4Q4s allocated there for the 309 we swapped with three 15T13s for the 318 group where certain duties required extra capacity.

On 18th May, there was a reorganisation of the CM routes. Route 408 was restructured so that it no longer needed five of its 4Q4s. The 403/A/B used them with the warning that single-deckers should not be used through to Tonbridge. At this same date, service 414 took on one official Monday-Friday Q working from RG for the shorts between Reigate and Dorking.

It is worth noting that during this period a number of well-known photographers began recording the scene in earnest. It is clear that the Qs were now being used to plug gaps on a number of trunk routes whether they were officially allocated or not. Even a quick check through my own collection shows that 4Q4s were to be found on the 402 group DG, 403 (DG as well as CM), 409 (EG and GD), 410 (GD and RG), 431 group (DG) and 480 (NF). It should not, of course, be forgotten that certain cross-workings were also scheduled. It is also apparent that at SA the 6Q6s allocated to the 355 route were also to be seen on the 342, 355, 365 and 382. At the time, the oldest double-deckers, essentially the STs were being withdrawn, or in some cases temporarily allocated to the Central Area, and replacements both STLs and brand new RTs were in short supply.

On 15th June, a new spur working between Smallfield and Home was introduced on the 424. It was considered more appropriate that this be worked by a Q from CY, so to balance duties, one of CY's on 434 was transferred to EG to allow for this.

New route 332 (Bushey Station-Cassiobury Estate) was introduced on 5th October. Red Q53 was transferred from TG to WA to work it. By now, 419 at LH had mainly returned to 4Q4 working whilst at NF the 497, which had returned to single-deckers with Ts earlier, now used 4Q4s again. The Country Area had a small surplus of Qs. Relief work on the Green Line network still employed some Qs, Q39 allocated to WR was a regular Green Line duplicate for some years, WR otherwise not operating the type. In the summer months, K borrowed 4Q4s at weekends for heavily used local Kingston services. The class was undergoing another overhaul cycle throughout the year. But on 1st December, eleven buses were delicensed; Q6, 16, 186 NFu, Q10,21 EGu, Q13 RGu, Q14 DGu, Q15,20 CMu, Q34 SAu, and Q198 GFu. A number of transfers within the class also occurred to make up numbers.

Finally on 12th December, Q46 (ex NF) Q93 (ex WT) and Q94 (ex RG) were transferred to Swanley Junction (SJ) where they took up temporary service on 478 (Swanley-Wrotham) replacing Ts. This however was short-lived as the route was double-decked on 6th February 1950 with STLs. Q93/4 then moved from SJ to NF to replace Q44,65 which left the Country Area.

1950–1953

On 23rd January 1950, 4Q4s Q35 and Q59 moved into Kingston (K) as trainers. The Central Area's need for further single-deckers had become so severe that they could not afford to be pernickety over what they were offered. In fact, K was the obvious choice for the operation of 4Q4s, and it was strange that the idea had not been thought of earlier. After all, the type was regularly borrowed from RG each summer weekend to duplicate the local services.

Furthermore, many of the K routes going out into the Surrey countryside as they did served territory very similar to that which the 4Q4s normally operated in. On 6th February Q44,65 were transferred to K and Q8 followed on 4th March. QIO/3/5/6,53,85 arrived on 26th March and, exactly a month later, Q6 and Q20. Q21 and Q67 arrived on 1st May and straggler Q26 on 6th June.

Q8,44,53,65 and 85 were still in their red livery from their previous incursion into the Central Area, and Q6, 16,20/1/6 were repainted red in the course of the year. The remainder operated in green throughout. The trainers however returned to the Country Area without seeing service.

Also, on 6th February, the 454/A at DG was completely converted to STL, previously having used one STL and one 4Q4. Q83 then moved from DG to NF. By no means all of the 4Q4s transferred to K were from the stored stock, and indeed often compensatory transfers were necessary. For example, when the only l/4Q4/l to be sent to the Central Area Q85 moved from TG to K presumably because it was red, Q34 was then relicensed. to TG on 26th March.

Relatively recent route 332 was amended on 7th June when it was extended to Oxhey Estate. The opportunity was taken to introduce STLs and the solitary 4Q4 was no longer required for the service at WA.

The Country Area winter programme on 27th September provided for a reorganisation of routes in the · Addlestone area, particularly to restore links in Woking which had been lost in the 1943 changes. The delivery of RLHs to GD to replace the lowheight 'Godstone STLs' gave an ideal opportunity, for these buses still had some life left in them. The scheme was wide ranging but as far as the Qs were concerned, route 436B was withdrawn and replaced by an extension of 463 (Walton-Woking) to Guildford via Merrow. 438 was also replaced by extending 436 (Staines-Woking) to Guildford via Burpham. 436A (Ripley-Woking) was extended to Staines. Double-deckers were used meaning that six 6Q6s were no longer needed at GF, three from 436B, two from 438, and one from 436A.

This set off a chain of transfers: Q199,216/28/31/4/7 moved from GF to SA which already used the 6Q6 on the 355, and they were also now freely to be found on 365,391/A group as well as 382 and covering the four special duty Qs at the garage. 4Q4s Q76,80 were transferred to WT, and Q48/9,50/4,64 moved to DG where Ts were replaced on 404 (Shoreham Village-Sevenoaks), 413 Chipstead-Brasted), 413A (Chipstead-Four Elms), and 421 (Heverharn-Sevenoaks), as well as providing cross-working journeys on 402, 403 and 431 group. The schedules were: 404 4Q4 1/1/1, 413/A 4Q4 2/2/2, and 421 4Q4 2/2/1.

The Allocation Books do not identify these changes either at SA or DG although the vehicle movements described together with Alan Cross's photographic record are clear on the point.

On the same day, route 316 (Chesham-Adeyfield) was converted from double to single-decker, initially with Ts. However, the 15Tl3s with their 31 seats were clearly not suitable, and on 16th October T789/92 were swapped with WT's Q76,80 for the two bus HH allocation.

1951 proved to be one of the quietest years for the Q class. The 4Q4s were falling due for their seventh overhaul cycle, and indeed a number had been attended to in 1950. Q24 emerged in January 1951, and then the cycle was halted. The 6Q6s had, of course, been operating as ambulances throughout the War, but a further cycle had commenced for them too. However, when Q189, and Q221 were completed in February 1951, no more were dealt with.

The usual reliefs were provided by RG at summer weekends for K and Green Line duplicates were also needed. There were examples allocated to garages as backup which did not normally use the type: 4Q4s Q45/7 to HG on 20th June, Q186 to WR on 8th August, and Q14 to LS on 13th August. On 17th October, Q27 and 41 were sent to GF for 432, and Q189,201 increased the number of 6Q6s at SA to compensate. Odd examples were delicensed as necessary.

The last new routes ever to receive an allocation of 4Q4s were 438 (Crawley-East Grinstead via Gatwick Airport) and 438A (Crawley-East Grinstead via Three Bridges) introduced on 30th April initially as Monday-Friday services. They had, in fact, been acquired from Sargeants of East Grinstead. Crawley had been designated a New Town, and growth required expansion of the bus services. Q36,40 were licensed at CY for the purpose.

Books and articles covering this period are usually biased to the Central Area, and the accounts of green bus operation are scant and badly researched. This is certainly the case for the demise of the Q class. The first Q to be withdrawn permanently from passenger service was Q217 from HG on 1st September 1939 when, along with the rest of the 6Q6s, it was converted to an ambulance for the Central Area. However on 18th July 1944, it was damaged beyond repair by a flying bomb whilst at Elmers End Garage (ED).

The first 4Q4 to be permanently withdrawn from passenger service was Q94 at NF when on 19th January 1951 it became a trainer at HG. Two TG 4Q4s, Q103 (1/10/51) and Q34 (27/11/51) were also withdrawn in that year.

By the start of 1952, new Green Line RF coaches were flooding in, and it was through the first six months of the year that the majority of the Qs were withdrawn. Apart from route 715 where 6Q6s were replaced by RFs, their replacement to routes was indirect. Green Line 10T10s (and TFs) which were downgraded to bus specification ousted not just Qs, but also 9T9s and 11Tl1s as well on a stop-gap basis until green Country bus RFs started to be delivered just over a year later. It was not that the Qs were inferior to the more conventional pre-war Regals, but rather that they had reached a time when a major overhaul would be needed and spare parts were no longer available. Indeed the withdrawn 6Q6s were still very serviceable such that they were stored rather than sold or scrapped, and as will be seen, many of them found further work in the Central Area.

On the very first day of 1952, Q192/7,203-5/8/11/2/4/5/22/5 at HG, and Q196,207/9/19/20 at GF were withdrawn and replaced by new RFs. Q200/24/9/30/3 (GF) followed on 9th January, and Q191 on 21st.

In what seemed a surprise at the time, Q198,206 (GF) and Q194,221,32/5 (HG) were transferred to Central Area garage Muswell Hill (MH) on 1st March, and Q238 (HG) followed five days later, all as trainers. It had been decided that the renovated LTLs were themselves becoming decrepit, and new red RFs were still some months away, so withdrawn 6Q6s should act as a stop-gap, on routes 210 and 244.

On 19th March Q191/4/8,200/3/4/6/8/l1/2*/5/6*/8*/21/2*/4/39/2/3/5/7*/8 entered service at MH replacing LTLs.

On 1st May, Q194/8,206/8/16*/20 were withdrawn for other non-passenger duties, and replaced by Q192,213*/25/9. On 10th September, new RF 289/91/3 entered service at MH, and Q191/2,224 were withdrawn. This process continued until 11th December, when Q230/8 were withdrawn and represented the last 6Q6s in passenger service. It should be remarked that the Green Line coaches received virtually no modification other than their doors being permanently fixed open to comply with Metropolitan Police requirement. Those buses marked * had in fact worked as buses in the Country Area before moving to MH.

The last 6Q6 to be withdrawn from Green Line duties was Q226 on 12th March 1952. The last Country Area 6Q6s to be withdrawn were Q190/3/5 on 16th April also at GF where their duties on route 432 were taken over by displaced 10T10s.

The other garage to build up a substantial allocation of 6Q6s for bus operation was SA. Q201/13/8 were withdrawn on 9th January, Q199,216 on 10th, Q202/7/10/3/23/36 on 16th, Q234/7 on 21st, and Q189,228 on 1st February. SA had a mixed allocation of 4Q4s and 6Q6s, and withdrawal of the 4Q4s took a little longer: Q81 on 10th January, Q100 on 1st February, Q98 on 12th, and the largest batch, Q82/4/7/9, 91/2/5, 102/87 on 25th March.

All the Q duties on routes 355,365,382,391/A as well as the extras at SA were replaced by underfloor engined Leyland TFs introduced in 1939, and mainly displaced from Grays (GY), whose busy East London 723 received new coach RFs. Indeed it was the Q and the TF with their unconventional engine locations which were the true predecessors of the underfloor RF, and not the mundane Regals with their engines at the front.

TG had already lost two of its 4Q4s in late 1951 when the main part of the service 387 had been converted to Cub with just one 4Q4 and, when Q68 was delicensed on 18th February 1952, a T was allocated to the big bus Monday to Friday operation.

There were several garages which had the odd 4Q4 helping out on relief duties and these were gradually flushed out: Q47 HG (1/2/52), Q76,80 HH and Q61 LH (18/2/52), Q41 GF and Q14 LS (1/3/52), and Q66 HG (12/3/52).

Q35,52/9,69,83,96 were withdrawn at NF on 1st March. (Q83 being one of the two examples preserved, although it had never been painted red!). Routes 489/A,497 were converted to Ts, although on 11th June, 497 was converted to double-deck with STLs.

On the same date, WT, at one time such a large operator of 4Q4s, delicensed Q57,88,90 and 104, which had worked duties on 309, 318/A to this point.

On 25th March, CM bid farewell to its 4Q4s which had remained faithful to the 453. Q58 was delicensed, but the remaining two saw service elsewhere, Q29 at EG, and Q105 at RG. Although 10T10s replaced them, an RT was already used on Sundays, and in February 1953, this was another route to be converted to double-deck operation. It was the turn of CY on 16th April. Q25,30/7,40/3/6,51,63,79 were withdrawn whilst Q70/2 moved to RG replacing delicensed Q24,97. Routes 424,426,434,438/A now used Ts.

There was a hiccup, however, in the conversion of EG. On the same date, Q11,29,48,55,60/2 were delicensed and 10T10s took over the 424 and 434. For some reason lost in the mists of time, this was not satisfactory, and all of the Qs were relicensed on 21st April, and it was T455,544/66/7/9/92 which were delicensed. On 1st May, all of the 4Q4s being Q7,11,22/8/9,55/6,60/2 were withdrawn at EG, this time being replaced by 10T10s from TG.

It was DG's turn to lose its 4Q4s on 1st June, when Q31,49,50/4,69 were delicensed and Q18 was transferred to Central Area at K replacing Q85, which had been withdrawn there ten days earlier. The Kent routes involved were 404,413/A and 421.

There was now only one garage in the Country Area with 4Q4s, and this was RG, which used them on 406C,439A,440/A and 447 /A/B. Journeys were also worked on 414 and photographic evidence shows that examples were also to be seen as substitutes on double-deck routes from the garage. In addition, it continued to supply K with weekend reliefs, especially through the summer period. From time to time, an example failed, was delicensed and replaced by another, one in store there and in better condition. Indeed, when on 1st February 1953, Q30 and Q43 were withdrawn and replaced from store by Q55 and Q79, it is likely that this event was responsible for Q55 being chosen as the example of the class to be preserved after it was finally withdrawn.

The 4Q4s at K continued and their withdrawal was gradual as replacements were released around the fleet, mainly TDs, which directly or indirectly had been displaced by the delivery of new red RFs at SP and MH. The Qs continued to the end with a mixture of green and red (+) examples. Q85+ was withdrawn on 20th May 1952, and replaced by Q18. On 19th August, Q10 and Q20+ were withdrawn, and a few days later replaced by Q42 and Q64 ex store.

The following winter they were withdrawn as follows: Q6+,8+,26+ (20/11/52), Q13,16+,21 + (1/1/53), Q65+ (21/1/53), Q53+ (1/2/53), Q67 (4/2/53), Q12,44+ (12/2/53), Q15 (1/3/53), Q18 (18/3/53) and Q42,64 (25/3/53). Interestingly, the last examples were still in the green livery.

The RG 4Q4s were the only Qs to be directly replaced by Country Bus RFs when the first examples, commencing with Rf 514, were allocated there. Q9,19,22/8,55,60,72/3/9,99 were withdrawn on 7th April 1953, and Q23,70/l,86,97,105 were withdrawn on 9th April. The class had lasted up to eighteen years, and despite their revolutionary design, had been the workhorses of Country Area Bus operation in addition to, at times, providing both Green Line and Central Area support. The class had bridged the period between the mixed bag of saloons inherited from London General Country Services and a motley selection taken over with independent operators, and the modem fleet of underfloor engined RFs which were to be the mainstay of the Country Area of the London Transport Executive for the next two decades, and indeed well into the NBC era of the Seventies after the divorce with London Transport.

Qs operated at some time or the other from almost all of the Country Area garages. In most cases they were scheduled. In a few instances, Qs were never scheduled, although odd examples were allocated as reliefs and spares. However, there is one major Country Area Garage which apparently never operated a single-deck Q, that being Grays (GY). Coincidentally, double-deck examples were allocated for a few weeks when, on 1st July 1939, Q2,4,5 were transferred from HG, and Q3 on 1st August 1939, also from HG before they were stored never to see further passenger service with London Transport.

It should also be recalled that for part of the period, a batch of Central Area 5Q5s painted green supported the Country fleet, as indeed in their last few months, a batch of 6Q6s repaid the compliment to the Central Area.

A number of the 4Q4s were dismantled and their bodies burned at Chiswick beginning with Q14 on 14th April 1952. Q69 was sold to the Gravesend Old People's Welfare Committee. Many more were sold to dealers as was the case with the 5Q5s and 6Q6s. A few even found their way abroad to places such as Cyprus, Malta, Yugoslavia, Libya and Rangoon.

There were several 'last days' for the Qs in 1952 and 1953 culminating on 9th April 1953 when the very last 4Q4s were withdrawn. I am unaware of any contemporary enthusiasts' celebrations, although advance information of such events would have been difficult to obtain at the time. It is less forgivable that 2002 and 2003 were allowed to pass without acknowledgement of the half century anniversary of the going of this invaluable class, or indeed that 2005 and 2006 should slip by with their seventieth anniversaries of the introduction of the 4Q4s, 5Q5s and 6Q6s being registered in the bus historian's mind.

2010 is the 7 5th anniversary of the entry into service of the first 4Q4s, and 2011 for the 5Q5s and 6Q6s. Perhaps, apart from this publication, some celebration of these unique vehicles would be appropriate.

I would like to express my gratitude and appreciation to Dennis Cox and Laurie Akehurst for their helpful comments after reading through the draft, and to George Seward for retyping my original manuscript.

Tailpiece: Ancient and modern meet up in Oxford Street early in 1937. Many LTs and STLs are visible in this busy scene, but Guildford's Q 194 is being closely followed by NS 2246 which, despite now being fitted with pneumatic tyres and a covered top, clearly represents an altogether earlier era in public vehicle design. Within six months NSs will be swept away from route 13 by the arrival of new STDs and not long afterwards, in November 1937, the class will become completely extinct.